Cognitive Conflict in Science:

Demonstrations in what scientists talk about and study.

Dissertation
der Mathematisch-Naturwissenschaflichen Fakultat
der Eberhard Karls Universitat Tübingen
zur Erlangung des Grades eines
Doktors der Naturwissenschaften
(Dr. rer. nat.)

vorgelegt von

Brett Buttliere, M.Sc., B.A.

aus Oak Brook, Illinois

Vereinigte Staaten

lbingen

2017

Gedruckt mit Genehmigung der Mathematisch-Naturwissenschaftlichen

Fakultät der Eberhard Karls Universität Tübingen.

Tag der mündlichen Qualifikation: 15.12.2017

Dekan: Prof. Dr. Wolfgang Rosenstiel

1. Berichterstatter: Prof. Dr. Friedrich Hesse

2. Berichterstatter: Prof. Dr. Sonja Utz

Table of Contents

Summary --

The concept of cognitive conflict, that being two competing ideas in the mind at the same time, encompasses a large number of instantiations throughout Psychology (Festinger, 1964; Heine, Proulx, & Vohs, 2006), even playing an important role in many philosophies considering how science works best (Kuhn, 1962; Platt, 1964; Popper, 1934/ 2005). This experience of cognitive conflict is widely considered to be aversive, but also motivating, for individuals across a wide range of contexts. Here I examined two ways cognitive conflict affects what topics receive scientific attention. Pairing the philosophies of science with Festinger's (1950) hypotheses about informal social communication, it was hypothesized that:

1. Scientists will discuss things they disagree about more than things they agree about.
2. Scientists will study more those topics which threaten individual or group outcomes.

Utilizing publicly available data about scientific publications, I tested these hypotheses within a number of contexts, including public comments on papers, Tweets about papers and topics, and the author and automatically generated keywords describing scientific papers themselves (as a measure of what scientists write about and study). Two studies suggested that more negations in the texts (e.g., but, not, however) were related to larger discussions, more views, and more media attention. Two other studies examined the keywords describing papers, first all papers published across science by PLoS, and then all papers across publishers within Psychology. Both studies suggested that there are more unique negative keywords studied, and that these keywords have more papers written about them, on average. Overall, the results suggest that scientists talk more when they disagree, and that they speak more about threats to the group and individual. This more generally implies that cognitive conflict plays a role in determining what scientists talk about and study, and more generally that general psychological principles can be applied within the context of science.

Zusammenfassung --

Das Konzept des kognitiven Konflikts, welches zwei gleichzeitig konkurrierende Ideen im Gehirn beschreibt, ist in der Psychologie häufig anzutreffen (Festinger, 1954, Heine, Proulx & Vohs, 2006) und spielt auch in der Philosophie eine wichtige Rolle, z.B. bei der Frage, wie Wissenschaft am effektivsten funktioniert (Kuhn, 1962, Platt, 1964; Popper, 1934/ 2005). Das Erleben eines kognitiven Konflikts wird in einer breiten Plaette von Kontexten weithin als aversiv und motivierend für Einzelpersonen betrachtet. In dieser Arbeit habe ich zwei Wege untersucht, wie kognitive Konflikte die wissenschaftliche Aufmerksamkeit auf Themen beeinflussen können. Durch eine Vekrnüpfung wissenschaftstheoretischer Philosophie mit Festingers (1950) Hypothesen über die informelle soziale Kommunikation wurden die Vermutungen aufgestellt, dass:

1. Wissenschaftler mehr über bestimmte Themen diskutieren, wenn sie darüber nicht mit anderen Wissenschaftlern übereinstimmen

2. Wissenschaftler jene Themen mehr untersuchen, die für das Individuum oder die Gruppe konflikthaft (im Sinne von bedrohlich) sind.

Durch die Nutzung öffentlich zugänglicher Daten über wissenschaftliche Publikationen habe ich diese Hypothesen in einer Reihe von Kontexten getestet, darunter die Kommentare zu Papieren, Tweets über Papiere und Themen sowie die von Autoren generierten und automatisch generierten Schlüsselwörter, welche die wissenschaftlichen Papiere beschreiben. Zwei Studien deuten darauf hin, dass mehr Negationen in den Texten (z. B."but"," not", „however") zulängeren Diskussionen, mehr Aufrufen der Papiere und zu mehr Medienaufmerksamkeit führen. Die beiden anderen Studien untersuchten zunächst alle Papiere, die in sämtlichen Disziplinen in der Zeitschrft PLoS veröffentlicht wurden, und dann alle psychologischen Papiere, wobei sich zeigte, dass es mehr einzigartige negative Schlüsselwörter gibt, und dass über diese Schlüsselwörter im Durchschnitt mehr Papiere geschrieben werden. Insgesamt implizieren die Ergebnisse, dass der kognitive Konflikt eine Rolle dabei spielt, welchen Themen sich Wissenschaftler zuwenden und worüber sie reden, und allgemeiner, dass die allgemeinen psychologischen Prinzipien auch im Kontext der Wissenschaft gelten; und insofern dass die Psychologie genutzt werden kann, um die Art und Weise zu verbessern, wie Wissenschaft durchgeführt wird.

Page left blank intentionally.

List of thesis related publications

- Buttliere, B., & Buder, J. (2017). Personalizing papers using Altmetrics: comparing paper 'Quality' or 'Impact' to person 'Intelligence' or 'Personality'. *Scientometrics*, 111(1), 219-239.
- Buttliere, B., & Buder, J., (In prep). When 'negative' comments are good for paper outcomes. Papers with comments receive more Academic, General, and Media attention.
- Buttliere, B., Buder, J., & Costas, R., (In prep). More discussed scientific topics are more contradicted.
- Buttliere, B., Zviagintseva, K., & Buder, J., (In prep). Scientists study more negative topics, more often.
- Buttliere, B., & Buder, J., (In prep). Evidence for a negativity bias in psychological science.

Other thesis related publications and presentations.

- Buttliere, B. (2017). The role of Cognitive Conflict in what scientists work on and talk about. *IWM Doctoral Colloquium Series*.
- Buttliere, B. (2017). A psychological science: The hidden dependencies of Altmetrics. *Workshop of the 4th Altmetrics Conference, Toronto, Canada*.
- Buttliere, B., Buder, J., & Costas, R., (2017). More tweeted scientific topics are also more negated. *4th Altmetrics Conference, Toronto, Canada*.
- Buttliere, B. & Buder, J., (2017). Evidence for a negativity bias in psychological science. *DFG Media Psychology Conference, Landeau, Germany*.
- Buttliere, B. (2016). The role of Cognitive Conflict in what scientists work on and talk about. *KMRC Doctoral Colloquium Series*. 30 minutes available here.
- Buttliere, B. (2016). Cognitive Conflict in Science. *Poster*
- Buttliere, B. (2015). The point of impact, or: How to change the world. Science slam presentation at the conference of the DGP Media Psychology Division. *Tübingen, Germany*.
- Buttliere, B. (2015). Identifying high impact scientific work using Natural Language Processing and Psychology. *WebSci15, Oxford, England*.
- Buttliere, B. T. (2014). Using science and psychology to improve the dissemination and evaluation of scientific work. *Frontiers in Computational Neuroscience, 8*.

Other publications, book chapters, and presentations

- Buttliere, B., & Buder, J., (2017). Reading more vs. writing back: Situation affordances drive reactions to conflicting information online. *Computers and Human Behavior*.
- Buttliere, B., & Buder, J., (2016). Reading more vs. writing back: Situation affordances drive reactions to conflicting information online. *WebSci15, Hannover Germany*.
- Buder, J., Buttliere, B., & Cress, U., (2017). The role of cognitive conflicts in informational environments: Conflicting evidence from the learning sciences and social psychology? In J. Buder & F. W. Hesse (Eds.), *Informational Environments: Effects of Use, Eeffective Designs* (pp. 53-74). New York, NY: Springer.

Other associated projects

- Buder, J., & Buttliere, B. (in preparation). Confirmations and Disconfirmations, rectifying the record.
- Holtz, P., Buttliere, B., Gnambs, T., (in preparation). Sentiment in the abstracts of scientific works.
- Yenikent, S., Holtz, P., Buttliere, B., Kimmerle, J. (in preparation). Sentiment and editor activity in Wikipedia titles.

1.0 Introduction

The goal of the dissertation is to examine the role of cognitive conflict within the context of science, providing evidence for Festinger's (1950) hypothesis that people talk and study more things that they disagree about, and things that are threatening to the individual and group. While incremental, it provides evidence for several interesting propositions, such as that scientists are humans, and that we can utilize the psychological literature to better understand how science works, and utilize how science works to tell us something about psychology. The theory is rooted in the idea that humans in general are motivated to reduce or avoid threatening stimuli (e.g., violence, disease, stress), and that science is at least in part a manifestation of this deeply rooted desire to avoid the bad and approach the good (Kuhn, 1962; Maslow, 2004; Popper, 1934/ 2005). This basic motivation to understand, and then use this understanding to achieve our best outcomes or desires, is the basic motivation behind all of our (formal) educative, religious, and, yes, even scientific enterprises.

Despite its important position, the basic role of cognitive conflict in science is almost never stated explicitly; either in theoretical discussions of what science is or how it should work; Kuhn describes the conflicts as anomalies, while Popper simply talks about being falsifyable (e.g., Kuhn, 1962; Popper, 1934/ 2005; Maslow, 2004). Even calls for suggestions on how to improve the way science is done hardly discuss the role of cognitive conflict (Bekkers, 2012; Birukou et al., 2011; Björk, 2007; Giner-Sorolla, 2012; Ioannidis, 2005; OSC, 2015; Simmons, Nelson, & Simonsohn, 2011), despite the fact that they themselves are motivated by a discrepancy or conflict between how they think science should be done and how it is done (Buttliere, 2014). Identifying and understanding the role that cognitive conflict plays in science will lead to a more efficient science, but also needs concrete, powerful, examples and demonstrations of conflict within the context of science. To provide such examples is the goal of the thesis.

1.1 Improving science

There have been in the last decade many attempts to better understand and increase the efficiency of science (Birukou et al., 2011; Björk, 2007; Giner-Sorolla, 2012; Ioannidis, 2005; OSC, 2015; Simmons, Nelson, & Simonsohn, 2011). This is a reasonable goal, given that over 473 Billion, generally public, dollars were spent on Science, Research, and Development in 2016 in the US and another 409 Billion dollars were spent in China during the same time (Wikipedia, 2017). There have been many attempts to improve *how* scientists answer their questions (e.g., preregistration, replication, higher power, better reporting, open data, open materials; LeBel, Loving, & Campbell, 2015), but almost no discussion of how scientists can ask better questions in the first place. Here, the goal is to motivate scientists to ask better questions in the first place by providing some first data that humans and scientists pay attention to the uncertain or potentially threatening stimuli. It is my assertion that focusing on and identifying areas of uncertainty or threat, and working to close them, is the very goal of science and will lead to good outcomes both for the individual and the group.

1.2 Studies of how science *should* work

This is not the first study to examine how science might work best, it is not even the first study focusing on anomolies (Kuhn, 1962) or putting theories against each other (Platt, 1964), but it will be one of the first utilizing empirical evidence from actual scientists to show that this is the case. Thomas Kuhn's *Structures of Scientific Revolutions* (1962) is perhaps the most prominent study on the topic, where he looked throughout the history of science and found that the newest and most brilliant ideas are often highly contested and controversial, starting out as 'anomalies' and even assumed to be some sorts of errors. Popper's (1934/ 2005) Logic of Science puts criticism and trying to prove each other wrong at the heart of his ideas on how science should work, and Platt's (1964) Strong Inference consists of explicitly identifying places where theories are in conflict and testing that spot until an answer is found.

These books and theories are great, and I would suggest all to follow their advice (especially those looking to do good science or improve how science is done), but they are not strongly rooted in theory, often ignoring the human in the scientist; and are not really empirical, rather being surveys of historical examples or prescriptions of how science should work. Even when authors empiricize these claims, as in a survey of Nobel Laureates, where they openly discussed their experiences of ridicule and rejection, relies upon memory biases and has a very small sample (Campanario, 2009). There is a nice study from Radicchi (2012) where he found that papers with formal comments on them were more likely to be in the top 1% of papers from their respective journal in terms of citations (Radicchi, 2012). Unfortunately, Radicchi (2012) offered no empirical evidence that these comments were actually negative, rather simply asserting that they were, and again Radicchi (2012) basically ignores the psychological foundation for the effects he discusses. That these ideas are not really empirically demonstrated might explain why they have limited impact on how science is actually done; scientists use mostly confirmatory strategies and avoid situations where they might be suggested or shown to be wrong (Gorman, 1984; Klayman & Ha, 1989; Wason, 1960). Here the goal is to, specifically in the next sections, root these ideas in the psychology of the scientist and then provide some empirical evidence that this is the case.

1.3 The psychology in the science

While there hasn't been much research on specifically cognitive conflict in science, a growing field is recognizing that the psychology of the scientist can be examined utilizing the same systems and constructs we do for 'normal' humans (Feist & Gorman, 2012). One of the most fundamental truths about the psychology of life in general, humans, and scientists in particular is that they attempt to develop true and useful meaning frameworks, which they then utilize to achieve their goals (Festinger, 1962; Heine et al., 2005; Kuhn, 1962; Nesse, 1990; Popper, 1934/ 2005). Evolution selects for this meaning making function as our meaning structures are the essential thing we rely upon to navigate through the world toward our goals with (Cosmides & Tooby, 2000; Heider, 2013; Nesse, 1990). The building and shaping of these meaning frameworks is in fact the essential motivation behind all of our formal education systems, religions, and even the scientific method itself. While not empirical, Kuhn suggests the importance of these meaning frameworks within the context of science, saying that, "To reject one paradigm without simultaneously substituting another is to reject science itself." (Kuhn, 1962, p. 77).

A concrete example of how Psychology, these all pervasive meaning frameworks, and the drives to reduce cognitive conflict operate within the context of science is the now (in)famous 'file drawer,' where researchers put the experimental studies which did not work out as expected (Nickerson, 1998; Sterne, Egger, & Moher, 2008). This file drawer is essentially an instantiation of what psychologists call the 'confirmation bias', wherein authors and editors are confronted with an unexpected piece of information (in this case the unexpectedly negative result of their experiment) and then find a way to dismiss it as not worthy of further thought or publication (Festinger, 1962; Greenwald, Pratkanis, Leippe, & Baumgardner, 1986; Nickerson, 1998). A large psychological literature and even our own work suggests that one of the easiest ways for humans to deal with incongruent information is to dismiss it as of low quality or to avoid thinking about it in general (Buttliere & Buder, 2015; Byrne, 1971; Hart, et al., 2009). Another way psychology and the desire to avoid cognitive conflict operates is in how scientists design and test their hypotheses, that being to show that their hypotheses are right, rather than to disprove them (Popper, 1934/ 2005; Wason, 1960). Other, more general examples of these meaning frameworks within the context of science are how scientists assume work coming from high status departments is better (Mahoney, 1976; Merton, 1968) or how they expect better outcomes for themselves than could be expected by statistics alone (Tversky & Kahneman, 1971). Note that these examples are all negative or related to bad outcomes; things to be fixed.

1.4 Cognitive conflict in psychology and science

One of the most important aspects of our psychology, along with the meaning frameworks in general, is a concept commonly called cognitive conflict, also known as dissonance (Festinger, 1954), uncertainty (Sartre, 1943), absurdity (Camus, 1955), unexpected stimuli or meaning violations (Heine et al., 2006), anomalies (Kuhn, 1962), the unknown (Piaget, 1954), and by many other terms besides (Koffka, 2013; Moscovici, 2001). Most of these concepts are accompanied by a state of consonance, certainty, or equilibrium where the being is comfortable, and the conflicting information or stimulus is disrupting this comfort (Heine, et al., 2006).

This cognitive conflict is a fundamental part of our cognitive system, and as such spans across and interacts with nearly every known phenomenon in Psychology. For example, all of the dual-process models of attention rely upon conflict when they state that things run on autopilot until something unexpected happens, at which point we direct our attention there (Evans & Stanovich, 2013; Kahneman, 2011). This unexpected stimulus is the one that conflicts with our expectations and a large number of studies suggest that we attend to it in order to return to our state of equilibrium (Öhman, Lundqvist, & Esteves, 2001). Our emotion processes are another good candidate for demonstrating how cognitive conflict interacts with other concepts. If we do poorly on a test we expected to do good on, it feels bad; but if we expected to do poorly, it doesn't feel (nearly as) bad. The same is opposite, if we didn't expect to do good, the positive emotion is stronger than if we expected to do really good (Heine, et al., 2006). While these processes can be shown in many contexts, the goal here will be to show how these processes occur within the context of science. This cognitive conflict has been so important as to be suggested to drive individuals to avoid information or people which create cognitive conflict, in order to avoid the threat to their current meaning frameworks (i.e., confirmation bias; Byrne, 1971).

While this conflict or dissonance is generally posited as feeling bad, motivating the individual back towards consonance, the dissonant, conflicting, or threatening experience of *not* knowing something is posited as a necessary step in the process of learning something new (Piaget, 1955). Failure and disagreement are important, especially in science. Piaget discusses the need to first experience the feeling of not knowing, or lacking some knowledge, before one can learn something (Piaget, 1955). Within the educational setting, there is evidence from preschool to college and beyond, people and children learn better when they are also confronted with negative information rather than only positive (when their theory is disconfirmed, rather than confirmed; van Schijndel, Visser, van Bers, & Raijmakers, 2015). Wason's 2 4 6 (1960) task demonstrated that people generally confirm, while Klayman and Ha (1987) summarize the substantial subsequent experimental literature by suggesting that people should disconfirm, though they generally confirm.

These ideas are also discussed within the context of science, Kuhn (1962), for instance, discusses how a group of scientists comes to change their mind, suggesting that often scientists ignore unexpected experimental results, then putting much effort into demonstrating that they are errors. Only if the result persists, do the scientists begin to search for ways to explain both the traditional phenomenon and the new phenomenon, often leading to what Kuhn calls a paradigm shift. The psychological conflict can be seen throughout, both in trying to stick to the traditional thought in explaining the unexpected as an error, and then searching for a new, better fitting, paradigm when it becomes clear it will not be possible to explain away the anomaly.

Not just Kuhn suggests that some disagreement between scientists is good for discussion and truthfinding. For instance, the Socratic Method is based upon the idea of critical, cooperative, debate, in order to more generally identify the beliefs which do not lead to contradictions. Hegel's (1807) dialectic similarly relies upon critical debate between the thesis and the antitheses, which then comes to a synthesis. More modern conceptualizations of how science works also have focused on cognitive conflict, with Popper's (1934/ 2005) *Falsificiationism* and Platt's (1964) *Strong Inference* essentially calling for finding places where hypotheses are in competition and testing them until one of the hypotheses is essentially disproven. These ideas have been corroborated through many other historical reviews (Greenwald, et al., 1986) and even a few surveys of Nobel Prize winners, outlining times when future award winning and field changing works were first rejected and criticized by the author's peers (Barber, 1961; Campanario, 2009; Stent, 1972).

People seem to learn better from conflicting information, but still scientists generally avoid conflicting information. Experimental studies of how people test hypotheses, and how this leads to finding the correct answer (in a simulated, contrived, environment), suggests that people and scientists test their ideas in a confirmatory manner, trying to find places where they are correct, rather than where they or others are incorrect (Gorman, 1984). Evidence has shown that in fact scientists are no different than pastors in how they test hypotheses (Mahoney, 1977), despite that evidence suggests a positive relationship between disconfirming hypotheses and finding the truth (in this contrived environment; Rullo & Meloy, 2008). Beveridge devotes an entire chapter to the conservative nature of science in his book on *The Art of Scientific Investigation*; summarizing he says, "there is in all of us a psychological tendency to resist new ideas" (Beveridge, 1951, p. 105). Here one goal is to encourage scientists toward productive conflict, especially in discussing uncertain or threatening, controversial, topics, by showing that at least some forms of conflict are associated with better outcomes, in general.

1.5 This, a study in two parts

Given that this cognitive conflict interacts with essentially every psychological concept, we also expect it to interact with science. The goal of the rest of the dissertation is to outline literature and then provide evidence suggesting that scientists will mostly talk about things they disagree about, especially when they are relevant or threatening to group or individual outcomes (e.g., disease, racism, fear). These two prongs can also be thought about as the two major drives of science: those beings to reduce uncertainty and solve problems. We will investigate these ideas utilizing data about the interactions between real scientists and how they describe their work, operationalizing the conflicting or negative experiences both as explicit negations (e.g., use of words like "but", "not", "however", or "shouldn't") and as negative sentiment (e.g., use of words like "error", "disease", or "cancer").

Cognitive conflict in what scientists talk about

The first of the two areas of examination will be whether scientists talk more when they disagree, and whether this discussion is good for the outcomes of papers or not. The drive toward consonance with the environment makes it such that the individual and group will pay the most attention to those things that are perceived as being most unclear. This can be easily demonstrated in those scientific articles that are most attended to, which often are controversial for some reason or another. For instance, the Kramer, Guillory, & Hancock (2014) Facebook emotion manipulation study was the most discussed paper in 2014, while the most discussed papers in 2015 include questions about whether perfect antibodies exist, whether vaccinations cause autism, why cancer occurs, and whether psychology is reproducible or not (Altmetrics, 2016; Buttliere, 2017). While this controversiality is demonstrable anecdotally, the goal will be to systematize and empiricize these ideas utilizing sentiment and other text analysis tools.

This idea has been discussed for a very long time. Indeed, Festinger (1950) summarizes the role that cognitive conflict and the drive toward consonance (away from dissonance) plays in communication when he suggests that,

> "1a: The pressure on members to communicate to others in the group concerning "item x" increases monotonically with increase in the perceived discrepancy in opinion concerning "item x" among members of the group." (Festinger, 1950, p. 273)

While the idea has been there, the actual empirical evidence for this, especially within the context of science, has been hard to come by, as researchers had to rely on small group discussions. More recently, research has begun providing evidence for this notion, for instance, in the topics that are discussed by the news (Castillo, El-Haddad, Pfeffer, and Stempeck, 2014) or in online social networking websites (Chmiel, et al., 2011), which have been suggested to be driven by disagreement. Empirical work in this area suggests that, for instance, longer discussions in online forums are more negative, and that the most active forum users also tend to be more negative (Chmiel, et al., 2011). Negative posts have also been suggested to be longer, with negative Amazon reviews being viewed as more informative and useful than positive posts; they in turn also get read more (Chen, Ibekwe-

SanJuan, SanJuan, & Weaver, 2006; Sen & Lerman, 2007; Sobkowicz, & Sobkowicz, 2012). Research specifically closer to the domain of knowledge creation and exchange suggests that more controversial topics receive more edits and prompt individuals to write more (Yenikent et al., in prep). Our own research suggests that people are more likely to write back online when they disagree, and that they write more on average when they disagree (Buttliere & Buder, 2015). Thus, there is substantial evidence that cognitive conflict is productive and leads to more discussion, which assumingly leads to better outcomes for all (Osborne, 2010).

More than just individuals paying attention or responding, there is also evidence that the conflict attracts the attention of other scientists to the problem. Greenwald and colleagues (1986), in their discussion of when theories hurt our ability to interpret new information (they basically say when the information contradicts our theory), suggest about controversy that:

> "Careful analysis might reveal that ultimate resolutions of empirical controversies are more likely to be produced by theoretically impartial bystanders who were warmed to action by the flames of controversy than by theoretically committed antagonists." (Greenwald et al., 1986, p. 225).

While these ideas exist and are even widely believed, they are not really empiricized in a satisfactorily psychological manner. There is one study from Radicchi (2012) which suggests that papers with formally published comments on them are more likely to be among the top cited papers in their respective journals. This is a good first step, but they are formal comments (i.e., another paper citing the original) and there was no evidence or investigation whether the comments were actually negative or not, it was only assumed.

Thus, in this portion of the project, one of the main goals of the dissertation will be to examine whether discussion is good for the outcomes of papers, whether scientific discussion is negative, whether the amount of negativity in the comments on a paper is related to the outcomes of the paper, and whether more discussed topics, in general, are also more negated. The first project will do this by examining first the comments on scientific papers, to see if they are good for outcomes, whether they are actually negative, and whether the negativity or debate in these comments is related to the outcomes of the papers they are on. Guided by the results of the first project, the second project will examine more specifically whether the number of Tweets about scientific topics is related to the number of negations in those Tweets.

Negativity in the keywords scientists work on
The second part of the thesis will more specifically focus on the topics scientists write papers about, suggesting that scientists write more papers about topics which are negative or threatening to them or the group in general (e.g., disease, threat, fear). Uncertainty and disagreement is a threatening experience, but explicitly threatening stimuli and entities (e.g., bacteria, cancer, and infection) should be expected to be given more attention than their neutral or positive counterparts.

This hypothesis is supported by many studies suggesting that humans have a general negativity bias (Baumeister, et al., 2001). In large parts this is essentially the same as the first part, simply examining those topics that scientists write papers on, rather than their more informal discussion on the internet. But there is some literature bearing directly on these topics, for instance, it is taken as a law in behavioral economics that losses hurt more than equal gains, that this difference gets bigger as the losses do, and people are willing to work more to avoid a loss than equal gain (Kahneman & Tversky, 1979). Other research suggests that a single negative or threatening piece of information outweighs in importance other positive informations, even in babies (Byrne, 1971; Fiske, 1980; Hornik, Risenhoover, & Gunnar, 1987). In the news, it has been specifically shown that they are more likely to cover more negative topics (e.g., stock market loss than stock market gains; Diamond, 1978; Lengauer, Esser, & Berganza, 2012; Niven, 2001; Soroka, & McAdams, 2015).

I expect this negativity bias to demonstrate itself within the context of science, in scientists studying more varied negative topics, and paying more attention to those negative topics than similarly valenced positive topics. This is, in essence, testing Festinger's (1950) second hypotheses about informal social communication, that,

> "Ib: The pressure on a member to communicate to others in the group concerning "item x" increases monotonically with increase in the degree of relevance of "item x" to the functioning of the group." (Festinger, 1950, p. 274)

Groups (and individuals) will pay more attention to a topic when it is more relevant for the group functioning. Such can be evidenced especially well in the amount of discussion related to replicability is psychology, being the most discussed Psych paper of 2015 (Buttliere, 2017).

This hypothesis is again evidenced in the definition and goal of science, where science, especially when publicly funded, is expected to lead to problems being solved and a better life for all (Caldin, 1940; Maslow, 1966). Even though it is in essence part of the definition of science, the idea that science is essentially a problem solving enterprise, has not been strongly picked up by the philosophers, in the same way that they focused on disagreement (i.e., they said disagreement is important, but they didn't say the disagreement is more likely to be about topics that are relevant for the group).

One of the first indications of this idea within the context of science was Seligman and Csikszentmihalyi (2014), who asserted that psychology, in particular, has been focusing too much on the negative, the disorder, and argue for a more positive psychology. Aside that they did not provide any data to back up their assertion, one should ask whether such a positive psychology movement would even be good for psychology, if humans have a bias toward examining the negative, dangerous, or threatening, as is discussed in the literature.

The dissertation will examine this notion that scientists pay more attention to negative or dangerous stimuli by looking at the sentiment of the keywords utilized to describe scientific papers. Collecting the keywords of scientific papers allows the computer to count how many unique positive and negative terms are there, and because the computer can count how many times each of those unique keywords are used, approximate the size of the research field about that topic. It is hypothesized that there will be more unique negative keywords studied by scientists, and that the number of publications about these negative keywords will be statistically larger than the number of papers about neutral or positive keywords.

Data from the internet
More than just answering relevant and interesting questions, the next important way innovation is in the type of data we utilize to answer these questions. Most of the studies outlined above utilize either historical analysis or small samples of experimental data to suggest their conclusions. The problem here is that there is not so much ability to say something about people in general from such small samples. It would probably be entirely possible to have participants come to the lab and discuss, or to conduct a survey about the topics that scientists work on, and even many psychologists might prefer that approach to the one taken here. Surveys of scientists are good (my Master's thesis was one), but the demands on their time make it extremely expensive to get and even when they give you time to collect data, they often don't give very much time. More than this, there are always the demand and generalizability problems. With just a little bit of extra effort to learn how to tell the computer what we want it to do, vast stores of 'behavioral residue', that is, traces of scientists' behavior on the internet, become available to us for investigation. The most difficult question then becomes not how to get the data, but which of the many sources of data to use.

In the end I chose to use the Public Library of Science's Article Level Metrics (ALM) Application Programming Interface (API). This machine makes available a large amount of information about the papers PLoS has published. The API makes available, many types of data, for instance, the full text, keywords, author list, list of citations, journal, but also a large amount of meta information, including how many times it has been viewed, cited, saved, and discussed online. More than just the number of times it has been discussed online, the API allows one to see exactly what was said and who said it. For my purposes I chose to take as the beginning sample all those **32,962** papers that PLoS published during 2014. Later, to examine and empiricize more closely **Seligman and Csikszentmihalyi's (2014)** assertion that psychology in particular is negative biased, I utilized data from the Web of Science on all those papers published between January and October 2013 which utilized the field keyword of Psychology.

Computational and sentimental methods

Having these large datasets is only useful if one can functionally interpret them. Again, I could have had participants come to the lab and rate for instance the comments or tweets, on things like, controversiality, conflict, negativity, or many other metrics. But again this approach really limits the data can be involved or analyzed, and essentially takes it back into the lab. Especially when dealing with as large of data as will be handled here (e.g., 42,000 unique keywords), having participants or students hand code them is just not functional. For each keyword one would need at least five measurements, and even having participants rate ten, fifty, or even one hundred would take nearly 2,000 participants to reach even a doubtable indication of the keywords' sentiment. Having research assistants read the comments or keywords and come up with a way to categorize them is costly and again, simply not convincing. It also opens up that the students could not understand. It would be best to have actual scientists rating, but this is also simply not functional.

Thus, I utilized the existing expertise in identifying the sentiment or analysis of texts. In order to not rely on any particular expertise too heavily, I utilized three sentiment analyzers (one could think of them as separate coders), to best understand the negativity or conflict in the texts. The three sentiment analyzers are all well standardized and were chosen for their well respected positions in the research landscape. The first sentiment analyzer I utilized was one of the very first, simplest, and most straightforward sentiment analyzers to be developed (Hu & Liu, 2004). It essentially compares each word to a dictionary of words which have been previously determined through various means of testing, to be positive or negative. The second analyzer is the Linguistic Inquiry and Word Count (LIWC), which is the standard analyzer within psychology and developed by a past president of the Society for Personality and Social Psychology (Pennebaker, Francis, & Booth, 2015), and finally Sentistrength, which was developed in part by a bibliometrician and has been utilized for a wide range of tasks including science and bibliometric related tasks (Thelwall, Haustein, Larivière, & Sugimoto, 2013). While Hu and Liu (2014) and Sentistrength are basically sentiment dictionaries, LIWC makes available a wide range of dictionaries, including one for identifying the amount of negation (e.g., "but", "not") in texts. Making it even more concrete, in the second study I identified and named ten terms which were put forward as clear indicators of conflict, which even some of the analyzers removed as stop words (e.g., but, not). Those words consist of: "not", "…n't", "but", "wrong", "incorrect", "error", "problem", "however", "fight", "doubt", and "contradiction" that nearly always indicate conflict of some sort.

1.6 Executive Objectives and Outline

In sum then, the goal of the dissertation is to provide evidence that cognitive conflict, defined as two conflicting or contradicting ideas in the brain at the same time, demonstrates itself within the context of the scientific enterprise. Based on the empirical literature about our psychology (e.g., Festinger, 1950) and the philosophies of science (e.g., Kuhn, 1962), it can be expected that

> 1. Longer discussions, and more discussed topics, are also those that contain more negativity, contradiction, and debate; and
>
> 2. Scientists are more likely to study negative or threatening keywords, than neutral or positive keywords.

A summary of the studies is available in the table below, matching to their section in the dissertation.

Table 1: Outline of the Individual Projects, Organized Under Their Main Questions.

Dataset	Measurement	Outcome
2. More discussion, more disagreement		
2.1 Comments on papers	Negations, Sentiment	Outcomes of papers
2.2 Tweets on topics	Negations	Amount of discussion
3. More threat, more scientific attention		
3.1 Keywords in PLoS	Sentiment	Number and usage
4.2 Keywords in Psych	Sentiment	Number and usage

2. Cognitive conflict in what scientists talk about

In the attempt to demonstrate the role of cognitive conflict in science, I am examining two main hypotheses, the first being that scientists will talk more about what they disagree about, or things that are unclear and uncertain. In this regard, two projects were run. The first project examines whether comments on scientific papers are good for the outcomes of those papers (replicating Radicchi, 2012), and then whether the comments are actually negative or contain disagreement, along with examining whether those papers with more negative comments have better outcomes in the end. Learning some lessons from the first project, in the second project I more specifically focused on analyzing whether when there are more discussions started about a topic, there are also more negation terms (e.g., but, not, couldn't haven't) in those the first posts of the discussion. Overall, the results are generally consistent with the hypotheses, though there were also several unexpected findings and I learned several important lessons along the way. One thing I learned was that full texts can be problematic, thus I focused on keywords, rather than titles or abstracts, to more clearly operationalize the conflict and to measure what scientists work on, in the second part.

2.1 Are (negative) comments good for the outcomes of papers?

The first way I examined the role of cognitive conflict was in examining comments directly on the papers themselves, to see if the comments are negative and to see if this relates at all to the outcomes of the papers they are on. Previous research (Radicchi, 2012) has suggested that scientific papers with formal comments on them do achieve more citations, and that comments on papers are in general negative. Radicchi (2012) though, did not look at the actual sentiment of the comments utilizing any systematic approach. Thus, in this first, relatively exploratory, project, I aimed to replicate Radicchi's (2012) initial finding that papers with comments have better outcomes, and then submit the comments to several well tested and standardized sentiment analyzers to demonstrate the negativity in them.

Getting the sentiment of the comments opened up other questions that could be asked, such as: 1. whether the comments were, in general, negative (Radicchi, 2012). 2. Whether longer comments were more negative (Chmiel et al., 2011). 3. whether negative comments were more likely to get replies (Sobkowicz, & Sobkowicz, (2012). and 4. whether the negative sentiment in those comments was positively related to the outcomes of the paper they were made on.

2.1.1 Methodological overview and key results.

Thus, the goal here is to examine whether discussion is good for the outcomes of papers, whether this discussion tends to be negative or contain disagreement, and whether negative discussion is good for the outcomes of papers. In order to test these ideas, and as a base sample for the dissertation generally, those 32,870 papers published by PLoS in 2014, made available through the PLoS Article Level Metrics (ALM) Application Programming Interface (API). The PLoS ALM API makes available 24 base metrics, and then the ability to further break down those base metrics. An example of this breaking down of the base metrics will be apparent in this project, where we first take the number of comments about the paper (the base metric) and then go into the subinformation, where we extract the actual text, the number of replies, and then even the length of the texts and their sentiment.

Of the 32,870 papers published by PLoS, 1,292 have at least a single comment on them. Table 1 displays the frequencies of papers that have comments for the entire dataset, with the maximum of 38 comments on a single paper (titled *Critical Assessment of the Evidence for Striped Nanoparticles*). The goal of the study is then, first to relate the number of comments each paper has to its outcomes, and then to examine the content of the comments utilizing several well-known sentiment analysis tools, to see if they are negative; and finally to see if the negativity in the comments is related to the paper's outcomes.

The next major question, then, was to decide what outcomes were to be considered best and related to the number of comments on the paper. That the PLoS API makes available so much data is excellent in one way, but also the multitude of metrics makes analysis difficult (where to start?) and opens one to the criticism that I just ran everything and picked the best outcomes to report. In order to reduce the number of forking paths down the line, I factor analyzed these 24 metrics, finding that 3 'Attention' metrics best explained the larger dataset. While I won't discuss the work very much here, as the metrics only matter for the first study, the paper is a good explanation of why I focus on saying things like types of

'Attention', rather than 'Quality' or 'Goodness' of the papers, though I would argue that the attention is generally good. These metrics we created, and several additional thoughts on the topic, were published in *Scientometrics* (Buttliere & Buder, 2017), but essentially consisted of factor analyzing the metrics to see if there were underlying drivers and what they might be. My colleague and I found that they could best be explained as three types of attention: Academic Attention (comprising of 4 citation metrics), General Attention (Viewcounts, Mendeley Saves, and Twitter metrics), and Media Attention (Counts of links on blogs and news sites). These metrics are positively correlated at about .50, though the Academic and Media attentions were not found to correlate meaningfully ($r = .02$). Much more information about these metrics can be seen in the full paper (Buttliere & Buder, 2017), and this is the only time they are used in the dissertation, which is why we don't focus on them too much.

Analysis 1: Examining whether papers with comments receive more Attention.

The first step will be to replicate Radicchi (2012), in showing that papers with comments have more scientific impact than those that do not. In order to do this, I tested both whether those papers that have comments have better outcomes than those that have no comments, and whether more comments are related to better outcomes. The outcomes measures will again be the three Attention metrics from Buttliere & Buder (2017): Scientific Attention (mostly citations), General Attention (mostly view counts), and then Media Attention (mostly counts of media stories about papers).

Table 1
Number of Comments on the Entire Dataset.

N comments	0	1	2	3	4	5	6	7	8	9	10	11	13	14	15	21	30	31	38
N papers	31,578	954	229	49	29	8	3	4	3	2	2	2	1	1	1	1	1	1	1

Note: N = 32,870, With 1,292 Having One or More Comments.

Academic Attention

Examining whether those 1,292 papers with one or more comments on them are cited more than those 31,578 without comments, it was found that they are statistically different with papers with at least one comment having .36 standard deviations more Academic Attention, on average (b = .36; t = -12.47; p < .001). Finding that papers with comments have more citations than those without comments, I next examined whether the number of comments was related to better outcomes in general. The results suggest that each comment on a paper is worth approximately .10 standard deviations of Academic Attention or citations, on average (b = .10, SE = .01, F(2, 32868) = 9.88, p < .001)meaning about .25 more citations per paper. These results clearly replicate Radicchi (2012) in finding that those papers with comments on them receive more citations / academic attention. While these results are positive and interesting, it should be noted that the number of comments on the paper explains less than 1% of the variance in the Attention Metrics of the paper, though this is reasonable given the simplicity of the analysis and that so many of the papers had the same number of comments.

Table 2
Standardized means and t test results between those papers without any comments and those with at least one comment.

	No Comments	Comments	t value	df	p value
Academic Attention	-0.02	0.36	-12.47	1376	2.20E-16
General Attention	-0.04	0.90	-21.51	1327	2.20E-16
Media Attention	-0.04	1.07	-14.75	1299	2.20E-16

Note: N No comments = 31,578, N Comments = 1,292.

General Attention

Having found that those papers with comments receive more Academic Attention (replicating Radicchi, 2012), I also wanted to see if they also received more General and Media Attention. When predicting the number of views the paper receives, I found that having one or more comments on a paper is on average, related to having .90 of a standard deviation worth of views on a paper (approximately 3,500 views), on average (M no comments = -.04, M comments = .90; $t(32,869)$ = -21.51, $p < .001$). Looking linearly, each comment is worth approximately .38 standard deviations of views, or approximately 1,500 views per comment, on average ($b = .38$; $SE = .01$; $t(32868) = 36.71$; $p < .001$). Notably, the number of comments on the paper alone explains 3.9% of the variance in the number of views the paper receives.

Media Attention

Finally, I wanted to examine whether those papers with comments receive also more Media Attention. Again, I found that having one or more comments is good for the Media outcomes of the paper, with those papers with at least one comment having more than one standard deviation more media stories written about them (M no comments = -.04, M comments = 1.074; $t(32868)$ = -14.745, $p < .001$). Each comment on the paper is worth approximately half of a standard deviation of Media Attention for the paper ($b = .57$; $SE = .01$; $t(32868) = 56.91$; $p < .001$), which equates out to about 9 online mentions. Notably the number of comments on the paper alone explains 8.9% of the variance in the Media Attention paid to a paper.

Running all together

Thus finding that papers with comments on them receive more citations, more views, and more media attention, I wanted to examine which metric is most related to comments. Before examining the comments themselves, I also wanted to compare the relationships between number of comments and each of the types of Attention, while controlling for the other Attentions. The results are displayed in Table 3, the main effects suddenly become negative for Academic and Media Attention types, though there are also interactions which must be taken into account. The largest effect is a positive interaction between General and Media Attention, suggesting that the relationship between General and comments becomes stronger as one moves up the Media Attention scale; though there is a positive three way interaction across all three which is also a larger effect. This positive three way interaction suggests that the positive interaction between General and Media attention becomes even stronger when one moves up the Academic Attention metric. Notably, utilizing the three attention metrics predicts 14.7% of the variance in the number of comments.

Table 3

Predicting Number of Comments with the Outcome Metrics.

	Estimate	Std. Error	t Value	Pr(>|t|)	
(Intercept)	0.03	0.003	9.52	2.00E-16	***
Academic.Attention	-0.01	0.003	-3.28	0.00103	**
General.Attention	0.04	0.004	10.32	2.00E-16	***
Media.Attention	-0.08	0.006	-12.28	2.00E-16	***
Academic.Att:General.Att	0.01	0.003	2.85	0.00436	**
Academic.Att:Media.Att	-0.07	0.006	-12.91	2.00E-16	***
General.Att:Media.Att	0.06	0.002	39.45	2.00E-16	***
Acad.Att:Gen.Att:Media.Att	0.02	0.001	14.57	2.00E-16	***

Note. ***$p < .001$, **$p < .01$. Regression examining the relations between the three outcome variables and their interactions on the number of comments on the paper. Together, 14.7% of the variance in the number of comments on the paper can be explained utilizing the three outcome measures.

Summary at this stage

Thus far I have simply examined how having a comment and the number of comments there affect the amount of Academic, General and Media Attention a paper receives. I found that comments were positively related to all three of the outcome measures created in Buttliere and Buder (2017). In this sense the results clearly replicated Radicci (2012) in that papers with more comments get more citations. While Radicchi (2012) only examined citations as related to formal comments in a small number of general journals; here I replicated the effect across a much larger sample of papers, fields, and outcomes. While these results are interesting, one of the main tenants of the Radicchi (2012) paper was that those comments criticize the papers, they did not test this assumption in any way. Thus, the next step in the analysis was to collect the actual comments on the paper, and then sentiment analyze them, to examine whether the comments are actually negative.

Analysis 2: Are the comments negative?

Having found that those papers that have comments do better in terms of Academic, General, and Media Attention, I next wanted to examine whether the comments are actually negative or not. In order to do so, I gathered those 1,292 papers that had at least one comment on them and asked for the information the ALM API had about those comments. This new dataset included the title of the comment, its full text, the number of replies it received, an author id, author name, time, and the parent doi for each of the 1,626 individual comments (some papers had more than one comment).

As was outlined in the introduction, the goal was to test whether the comments were actually negative. Radicchi (2012) highlights some evidence in asserting that the comments are negative, but also a study conducted by Adie (2009) manually annotated comments on PLoS articles from the journal's inception to 2008 suggests that only 7% are direct criticisms. As previous work suggests that sentiment analysis can be functionally utilized on scientific discussion to rate the sentiment of citations, I examined the content in this sample (Sendhilkumar, Elakkiya, & Mahalakshmi, 2013).

The first step after collecting the data was to check for duplicate comments. The only ones that are logged as duplicates (25 of them) are form comments from the editorial staff correcting errors especially of editor affiliation. These duplicated comments were removed leaving 1,601 comments on the papers.

The sentiment of the texts

Having collected the comments and removed the duplicates, the next step was to extract the sentiment in the comments. In order to do so I utilized two commonly utilized sentiment analyzers; the Hu and Liu (2004) dictionaries and Linguistic Inquiry and Word Count (LIWC) tool from Pennebaker et al. (2015). Each sentiment analysis tool is cited more than 500 times. Both are clear and easy to understand, utilizing the dictionary approach, essentially comparing whether each word has been previously identified as a positive or negative word through various means of testing. Some of these ways include having people brainstorm category terms, comparing their usage in annotated texts, and being checked by experts. Whereas the Hu and Liu (2004) dictionary returns the raw number of positive or negative words, LIWC utilizes the percentage of words in the overall text that were a part of the dictionary. There is some question in how to combine the different metrics, and in order to keep it consistent with the Hu and Liu metric, I simply subtracted the percentage of negative words from the percentage of positive words, to see which occurred more frequently.

The overall sentiment for the comments from the Hu and Liu (2004) sentiment analyzer is .12 [-0.13: 0.34], SE = .12, t(1,598) < 1.5, p = .38. This is not statistically different from 0, but is, contrary to our hypotheses, positive. The data are extremely kurtotic (26.74), with more than 50% of the data being between -1 and 1. There are, on average, 3.29 negative terms in the texts and 3.4 positive terms in each text, with a .74 correlation between the number of positive words and the number of negative words in each text. This correlation might be simply because there are more words, but it is unclear at this time. The maximum score number of negative words in a text was 91, with the maximum positive score being 95.

The overall sentiment according to the LIWC analyzer is 1.04%, indicating that there are 1.04% more positive words than negative words in the texts. This is significantly different from 0, 1.04 [0.84; 1.25], SE = .01, $t(1598)$ = 10.0, p < .001), again suggesting that the texts contain more positive terms than negative terms. Examining the component scores from the LIWC output suggests that 2.09% of the terms in the comments are positive and 1.04% of the words in the comments are negative; indicating that there are approximately double the amount of positive words as there are negative words.

Another interesting scale that LIWC provides is a count of the number of negation terms in the texts (e.g., no, not, but, however). This metric is interesting as it gives an indication of how much explicit disagreement or negation is within the text, which might be a better metric than simply the positive or negative emotive content held within the text. Examining the results suggests that the comments have on average .87% [.79: .94] negation words, which is statistically different from 0, with a t value of 23.26, $df = 1,598$, and a p value below .001. While this metric indicates that there is at least some negation in the text, it is statistically lower than several other general samples of text which can be compared (e.g., 1.58%; Hancock, Landrigan, & Silver, 2007).

Overall, these results suggest that there is both positive and negative sentiment and negations in the comments, but that there is slightly more positive sentiment overall. While the Hu and Liu (2004) overall sentiment was not significantly different from 0, the LIWC analyzer returned a significantly positive overall average. This is surprising and against our expectations given the Radicchi (2012) and Adie (2009) studies.

Analysis 3: The relationship between sentiment and length of comment.

While the sentiment of the comments was found to be neutral or even slightly positive overall, I was also interested in testing whether the sentiment in the text was related to the length of the text, as predicted by Sen & Lerman (2007). This length of the comment will be taken as a measure of the time and effort the individual put in, in essence as measure of motivation (Festinger, 1950). In this way I can test the hypothesis that conflict (negation, negative sentiment) motivates people to put more effort into their comments, in the same way we expect the dissonance to motivate people to start studying or talking about the paper in the first place.

Counting the number of words in the texts suggests that the average comment has 177 words ($SD = 323$), with 1,067 characters ($SD = 444$) in total (including spaces and punctuation). The longest comment was 4,425 words, which is long enough to be its own paper. Both metrics, as might be expected, are positively skewed (5.78) and kurtotic (49.81); in order to correct these biases, the scores were logged and standardized. The word and character counts are correlated at .99, regardless of whether we utilize the raw scores or the logged and standardized versions (Kendall's rank correlations for the logged scores). I utilized the standardized word count metric because it is a compromise between the number of words in the text (as compared to number of letters and punctuation) and is better for the statistics.

After obtaining a normalized word count for each of the texts, I ran the simple correlations between the sentiment metrics and the length of the comments. The first column of Table 4 shows the raw correlations between the standardized number of words and the text variables I have examined thus far (in order of their introduction); all correlations above .05 are significant at the .05 level. The largest correlations are between the positive and negative sentiment scores from Hu and Liu (2004) at .66 and .64, respectively. One interpretation of these data could be that more emotions are motivating in general, and that longer comments are more emotional; but it is more likely the case that just because there are more words in general, there are then also more emotion words. This more nuanced understanding is supported by the overall sentiment score from Hu and Liu (2004) being correlated at -.04, which is only marginally significant ($t = -1.68$, $df = 1,597$, $p = .09$), even with the large sample. This is in the expected direction, but at |.04| not really of the magnitude I expected.

The correlations from the LIWC analyzer are significantly lower, as they already control for the amount of words in the text. Interestingly the LIWC positive sentiment metric is correlated at -.11, which is significant but again not really of the magnitude I was hoping for. There is no significant correlation between the percentage of negatively sentiment words and the length of the comments, though it is in the correct direction. The negation metric provided by LIWC has a 0 correlation with the length of the text, which is again a failure to replicate the general notion that disagreement motivates people, though I did find that there is less positivity in longer texts.

Table 4

Correlations Between Length of the Comment and the Text Analysis Scores

	1.	2.	3.	4.	5.	6.	7.
1. Nwords	1						
2. Hu & Liu Sentiment	-0.04	1					
3. Hu & Liu Positive	**0.66**	0.28	1				
4. Hu & Liu Negative	**0.64**	-0.44	**0.74**	1			
5. LIWC Positive	-0.11	0.12	0.05	-0.04	1		
6. LIWC Negative	0.03	-0.22	0.03	0.18	-0.05	1	
7. Negations	0.00	-0.01	0.02	0.02	-0.05	-0.01	1

Analysis 4: Sentiment, Length, Replies, and Outcomes

Having created and examined the relationships between the metrics of cognitive conflict, I next wanted to see how and whether these variables related to the outcomes of the papers. I will again run the analyses as we did in the first section, first predicting Academic Attention, then General Attention, and finally Media Attention. There are two major differences between the analyses from the last section and the first section. The first difference is that whereas in the first section I only utilized the number of comments on the paper, now I will utilize the number of comments, along with the metrics about the texts were created. The second difference is that instead of utilizing the entire 32,870 paper sample as in the first section, I now examine only those 1,292 papers that received a comment.

Academic Attention

Are the citation outcomes of papers with comments on them related to the length of the comments, the sentiment in those comments, the amount of negation words in the comments, or the number of replies to the comment? The results (in Table5) suggest not really. While all of the coefficients are in the expected direction, none reach significance and the overall explained variation is less than 1%. The positive sentiment metrics are the only ones with negative coefficients, indicating a negative relationship between the amount of positive sentiment in the text and the outcomes of the paper, but neither are significantly different from 0.

General Attention

While the academic outcomes of the paper seem to be generally unrelated to the sentiment in the text, the General Attention (i.e., Views, Tweets, Mendeley saves) appears to be quite related to the motivation variables I created (results in Table 5). As might be expected, the length of the comment, the number of replies the comments get, and the number of negation terms in the comments were all positively and significantly related to the General Attention the paper receives. The sentiment metrics, either positive or negative, were not significantly related to the outcomes of the paper. One difference is that in this case the positive sentiment metrics, they are also positive, rather than negative as might be expected; in any case they are not significant. Overall, the four metrics I created about the comments explain 5% of the variation in the number of views, tweets, and Mendeley saves the paper receives.

Media Attention

Similar to *General Attention*, it is the length of the texts, the percentage of negations in the text, and the number of replies that relate to the Media outcomes of the paper. Again the sentiment metrics are not significantly related to the outcomes of the paper. The largest predictor is whether the comments get responses or not, with a t value of 6.80 and a p value far below .01. These variables explain 6% of the variance in the amount of Media Attention.

2.1.2 Discussion

The results from this project were mixed. I did not find that the comments on scientific papers were negative, as was asserted by previous literature (Radicchi, 2012), nor did I find that longer comments in general were more negative, though I did find that among those papers with comments, those papers with longer comments, comments which received replies, and contained negation terms had better outcomes in terms of the General and Media Attention metrics (Buttliere & Buder, 2017).

That the sentiment results were not reliably related to anything was a surprise and there are several potential reasons for the surprising results. One suggestion I found in the literature during this time was that, in general text, there are actually more positive terms in the lexicon and that these terms are utilized more often (Pollyanna hypothesis; Boucher & Osgood, 1969). Another potential is that these generalized sentiment lexicons might not be the best for identifying conflict or disagreement between scientists. Examining the sentiment dictionaries more closely, I found that they contain things like cancer, stress, and tumor, rather than terms that indicate disagreement. Interestingly, the LIWC dictionary had the negation dictionary, and the more of these words the comments contained the better outcomes the paper the comment was on had, so that was interesting. Another problem with this analysis was that it only comprised of 1,626 comments, which is not really the power that I had in mind. Moving forward, I will try to find a larger dataset, and to more directly operationalize both the conflict metrics, and the topics, in order to get a better idea of what is being discussed about in science.

Table 5
Results Utilizing the Sentiment and Motivation Scores Predicting the Outcomes of the Papers

Academic attention

	Estimate	Std. Error	t	Pr(>|t|)	
(Intercept)	0.41	0.04	9.05	<2e-16	***
Number of Words	0.03	0.04	0.74	0.46	
Hu & Liu Positive	-0.01	0.01	-1.40	0.16	
Hu & Liu Negative	0.01	0.01	0.83	0.41	
LIWC Positive	-0.01	0.01	-1.20	0.23	
LIWC Negative	0.02	0.02	1.05	0.29	
LIWC Negate	0.00	0.02	0.20	0.84	
Number Replies	0.03	0.03	0.97	0.33	
R squared	0.00	7, *df* 1,590	1.06	0.39	

General Attention

	Estimate	Std. Error	t	Pr(>|t|)	
(Intercept)	1.12	0.08	14.18	2.00E-16	***
Number of Words	0.27	0.07	3.84	0.01	***
Hu & Liu Positive	0.00	0.01	0.10	0.92	
Hu & Liu Negative	0.00	0.01	0.13	0.90	
LIWC Positive	0.02	0.01	1.41	0.16	
LIWC Negative	0.02	0.03	0.77	0.44	
LIWC Negate	0.09	0.03	2.84	0.01	**
Number Replies	0.33	0.06	5.79	8.39E-09	***
R squared	0.05	7, 1590	12.39	2.00E-16	****

Media Attention

	Estimate	Std. Error	t	Pr(>|t|)	
(Intercept)	1.39	0.14	9.78	2.00E-16	***
Number of Words	0.43	0.13	3.36	0.001	***
Hu & Liu Positive	-0.02	0.02	-0.87	0.38	
HuLiu Negative	0.02	0.02	1.22	0.22	
LIWC Positive	0.03	0.02	1.14	0.25	
LIWC Negative	0.08	0.05	1.43	0.15	
LIWC Negate	0.18	0.06	3.08	0.002	**
Number Replies	0.71	0.10	6.80	1.52E-11	***
R squared	0.06	7, 1590	14.22	2.00E-16	***

Note. ***$p < .001$, **$p < .01$.

2.2 Are more tweeted scientific topics more negated?

The purpose of this project was to examine whether scientific topics which are more Tweeted also contain more negations in the tweets about them, continuing the examination of whether scientists will talk more about things that they disagree about (testing Festinger 1950's first hypothesis). More than continue the study, the goal was to solve several of the problems that were associated with the first study, those being the small sample size, and the different lengths of the texts. By utilizing Tweets, I collected a much larger sample, which is generally constrained to 140 characters, solving the problem of simply having more negations because the text is longer (more sentences). In study 1, only about 5% of the papers had a comment and only about 1% had more than one comment on them (so I basically tested the significant 5% and 1%). Another way I will address this, aside from the larger sample of Tweets, will be to move from the single paper to the Microtopic level of discussion.

By moving from the paper to the Microtopic level, I was able to combine the papers into larger groups, thereby improving the ability to measure how the size of the discussion is related to number of negations in that discussion. These Microtopic classifications come from Waltman and Eck (2012), and place the publications into topics based upon their network of citations. Aggregating to the Microtopic level also minimizes the chance that unrelated things will affect the analysis. For instance, one much tweeted paper (Brown, 2015; not in the sample) contained a marriage proposal in the acknowledgments. People were tweeting about the proposal and if we had analyzed at the paper level, this would have affected the results. At the Microtopic level it will be averaged with the other papers about the same Microtopic, mitigating some of that potential for damage.

2.2.1 *Methodological overview and main results*

Here the goal is then to empiricize these notions, by examining this socratic dialectic also in the discussions amongst scientists on social media. In order to achieve such, I pulled all of the papers from the Altmetrics database concerning those papers published by PLoS in 2014. After cleaning the data some, I ended up with 162,233 English or Latin language Tweets shared about those 32,870 papers. This same sample has been the basis for several other studies of ours, outlined in Buttliere (2015a) and Buttliere & Buder (2017).

Here I examined these hypotheses utilizing tweets about scientific papers published by PLoS during 2014. The first step was to remove all those tweets which contained non-English characters. This was done in Excel, by sorting by the character vectors and removing those before and after the normal a to z.

The Microtopics

Utilizing the Microtopic system from Waltman and Eck (2012) we identified 1,961 unique Microtopics among the 162,233 Tweets. Each topic has an average of 82.72 tweets, with an *SD* of 224 tweets; the median Microtopic has 18 tweets and the most tweeted

Microtopic, about dinosaurs, has 4,244 tweets associated with it. The 20 most Tweeted

Microtopics are displayed in Table 6. These 20 Microtopics were Tweeted 34,749 times,

accounting for 21% of the Tweets in the sample. Already, without examining the

controversiality of the Microtopics, it can be seen that Brain Computer Interfaces, Extinctions,

Obesity, Sexual Harassment, Bullying, Mars, HIV care, Diets, and Cancer are among the most

tweeted topics in the data set (as descriptor keywords of the Microtopics). These results are

anecdotal evidence for Festinger's 1950 hypothesis that groups of people will discuss those

topics upon which they disagree.

Contradictions in the Tweets.

I next wanted to examine how much argument or discussion was happening in the

Tweets. In order to do so, I created a brief list of contradiction words, and counted how often

they occurred in each of the tweets. This list of 10 keywords contains "not", its contraction

"...n't", "but", "wrong", "incorrect", "error", "problem", "however", "fight", "doubt", and

"contradiction". This list essentially has the same terms on it as the Linguistic Inquiry and

Word Count subsection on contradiction. One notable aspect is that I converted any instances

of "...n't" into its own string that could be interpreted by the analyzer; this was done to count

contradictions like didn't, couldn't, wouldn't, or shouldn't, which would otherwise be left out.

The average Tweet contains .06 of a controversial term, with a standard deviation of .

27. This equates to about one in 20 tweets containing a controversial word, overall. In more

concrete terms, 6,232 of the 162,233 Tweets contained a controversial word, while 1,228

contained two of the words and 87 tweets contained three of the terms. The overall average of

.055 [.053; .056] is statistically different from 0 with a t value of 83.70 (df = 162,232). Many

of the two and three contradiction texts are combinations of 'but' and 'not', for instance,

'PLOSONE study http://t.co/Ofbm0YQXVN : In #stemcells debate, public knew candidate positions but not policy specifics http://t.co/raU1tal1qX' Another example that could be considered less controversial, but still suggests that something which people thought was correct is not, is 'Consumption of Green Tea, but Not Black Tea or Coffee, Is Associated with Reduced Risk of Cognitive Decline http://t.co/fuZ4x4jHhw'.

As my interest was in topics rather than individual tweets, the next step was to find the average number of contradictions per Microtopic. The Microtopics have .037 contradictions on average; this is a first indication, though not statistical, that those Microtopics which are larger contain more contradictions in them, as when those larger topics are only counted one time, the average goes down. Even with the significantly smaller sample size (1,961 compared to 162, 232), and the lower average, this .037 is still statistically different from 0, with a t value of 13.34 and a p value far below .001.

Having now an estimation of the Controversiality of the Microtopics, I decided to examine a bit more closely those Microtopics which were the most discussed (Table 6). As was found above, several of these most discussed Microtopics are controversial even just by looking at the labels of the Microtopics (e.g., obesity, gene sequencing, replication, sexual harassment). But what is most interesting about these data is that these 20 Microtopics are, on average, .583 above the mean in terms of controversiality, while the overall average for the microtopics is .03. Running a statistical test of these 20 to see if they are significantly different than the overall average returns a t value of 16.16; with an *SE* of .18, *df* of 19, this is considered extremely significantly by conventional standards, with a p value below .0001. This is now statistical evidence that these most discussed topics are also more controversial than the average Microtopic, again lending evidence for Festinger's (1950) suggestion that groups will discuss more topics they disagree about.

Table 6

The 20 Most Discussed Microtopics.

N Tweets	Std. NTweets	Label	Cont.	Std.Cont.
4,244	3.34	dinosauria, reptilia, squamata, theropoda, aves	0.01	-0.26
2,377	2.97	complex network, network, community structure, community, small world network	0.03	0.02
2,175	2.92	brain computer interface, bci, ssvep, motor imagery, movement	0.16	1.3
2,022	2.87	bacillus, bacillus thurin-giensis, bt cotton, subsp, bt maize	0.14	1.16
1,962	2.85	butterfly, species distribution model, lycaenidae, conservation planning, nymphalidae	0.09	0.58
1,896	2.83	gut microbiota, obesity, butyrate, short chain fatty acid, resistant starch	**0.10**	**0.7**
1,842	2.81	next generation sequencing, assembly, rna seq, cancer genome,	**0.09**	**0.62**
1,790	2.79	middle stone age, olduvai gorge, early pleistocene, sierra de atapuerca, rhinocerotidae	0.04	0.06
1,729	2.77	wolf, canis, white tailed deer, elk, brown bear	0.07	0.4
1,711	2.76	effect size, animal model, replication, psychological science, p value	**0.06**	**0.31**
1,576	2.71	sexual harassment, workplace bullying, bullying, mobbing, workplace harassment	**0.07**	**0.44**
1,519	2.69	bibliometric analysis, h index, impact factor, citation analysis, citation	**0.11**	**0.88**
1,507	2.69	mars, martian atmosphere, martian, venus, gusev crater	0.01	-0.23
1,434	2.65	microplastic, marine debris, beach, ghost fishing, ingestion	0.05	0.23
1,340	2.61	tursiops truncatus, bottlenose dolphin, dolphin, cetacea, whale	0.01	-0.21
1,221	2.55	hiv care, adherence, antiretroviral adherence, medication adherence, hiv stigma	**0.03**	**-0.06**
1,167	2.52	cancer cachexia, leucine, protein synthesis, acid, branched chain	**0.11**	**0.86**
1,130	2.5	digit ratio, 2d 4d, testosterone, evolutionary psychology, menstrual cycle	**0.38**	**3.3**
1,083	2.48	chimpanzee, pan troglodyte, cebus apella, primate, Madagascar	0.06	0.29
1,024	2.44	mediterranean diet, food frequency questionnaire, vegetarian diet, dietary patterns, ffq	0.15	1.27

Note. I have highlighted some that I feel are controversial even simply by the topic keywords (e.g., obesity, gene sequencing, replication, sexual harassment). On the right hand side are the average number of contradictions in the tweets and the standardized number of contradictions in the Tweets (compared to the .04 overall mean). Comparing these topics to the overall analysis suggests they are significantly more controversial than the average Microtopic, with an average of .468 and a t value of 2.95 ($df = 23$, $p < .01$).

Having looked at the most discussed Microtopics, I also looked a bit more closely at the most controversial Microtopics (Table 7). The 10 most controversial topics with more than 20 Tweets about them are displayed within Table 7. There are several reasons for choosing to include only those topics with more than 20 Tweets. First and most important is that the goal is to measure something about groups of tweets and one tweet is simply not enough. More important is that if a Microtopic with only one tweet about it contains one contradiction word, the overall average for the Microtopic is then 1, which makes it the most controversial Microtopic in the data set, and this is simply not realistic.

Choosing a lower limit of 20 tweets means that if one of those 20 tweets contains a contradiction in them, it will put it at the overall average at the Tweet level (.06) and just above the average for the Microtopics overall (.03). This is also born out in that if I utilize all Microtopics, 6 of the top 8 spots are Microtopics which were only tweeted one time but had one or two contradiction terms in them. The topic in 9th place overall (and most controversial topic with more than 20 Tweets), with 52 tweets about it and an overall Controversiality score of .90, concerns the Gender wage gap, occupational segregation, learning, inequality, and wage differential, which brings some face validity to the measure

The interesting analysis here is to essentially flip the analysis done above; asking whether those most controversial Microtopics are also discussed more. Where above there was convincing evidence that the most discussed topics were also more controversial than the average topic, this analysis would indicate that those most controversial topics with more than 20 tweets had more tweets on average than the rest of the topics with more than 20 tweets. In fact, I found that those 10 most controversial Microtopics, with an average of .58, $SE = .12$, is not statistically significantly different from the overall average of .85, $SE = .021$, and if anything lower than the overall average. This is contrary to my hypotheses, and if I examine the 10 most controversial Microtopics overall, indeed I find that they are statistically less talked about than the average Microtopic (as 8 of the top ten are tweeted less than 4 times; $t = 3.82$, $df = 1,959$, $p < .01$). Overall the results so far would suggest that being the most controversial might not be good for the outcomes, but still, the most discussed are controversial.

Table 7

The 10 Most Controversial Microtopics

Controversy	Controversy.std	nTweets	nTweets.std	Microtopicnames
0.90	7.00	52	0.58	**gender wage gap, occupational segregation, earning, inequality, wage differential**
0.71	5.47	21	0.02	intermittent exotropia, amblyopia, strabismus, myopia progression, chick
0.65	4.97	46	0.50	**american indian, aboriginal, indigenous australian, northern territory, inuit**
0.53	3.98	68	0.74	**indeterminacy, habit formation, precautionary saving, fertility, consumption**
0.46	3.41	87	0.9	lead electrocardiogram, electrocardiographic artifact, intensive care unit, hemodialysis, interpretation
0.45	3.31	132	1.16	**bipolar depression, pediatric bipolar disorder, acute mania, mania, lithium**
0.44	3.29	27	0.18	**alternative medicine, wort, complementary, homeopathy, john**
0.44	3.25	25	0.13	microtubule, water, delayed luminescence, self organization, biophoton emission
0.43	3.18	72	0.78	leber, mitochondrial dna, hereditary optic neuropathy, lactic acidosis, leigh syndrome
0.42	3.05	65	0.72	**mental rotation, sex difference, spatial ability, virtual environment, landmark**

Note: The ten most controversial Microtopics with more than 20 Tweets (to avoid those Microtopics with only 1 tweet from dominating). The results provide face validity to the metric of controversy, as the majority of the topics are controversial even by looking only at the labels, the coffee/ green tea example is one where a controversial claim is not as instantly obvious. Note that these are above the mean in terms of tweets about them, though note also that I removed all those with less than the mean, when I removed those with less than 20 tweets.

Relationship between number of Tweets and Controversiality

The main question of the analysis was whether Microtopics that were tweeted about more also had more contradictory terms in those tweets. In the overall data set, utilizing the raw, skewed data, the overall correlation is .05, with a t of 2.35 and a p value of .02, $df =$ 1,958. Examining the correlation utilized the logged and standardized data gives a correlation of .13, with a t of 5.7, across 1,959 Microtopics, and a p-value less than .001. This correlation is smaller than would be expected overall, but in the correct direction and significant.

Utilizing only those Microtopics with more than 20 tweets results in an increase in the raw correlation at .08, with a t of 2.31 ($df = 916$; $p = .02$). Utilizing the logged and standardized version of the data, the correlation is suspiciously similar to the correlation utilizing the logged and standardized data from the overall data set, at .13, but the result is correct and it only has the proper 916 Microtopics in the analysis, the p value is still far below .001. I also, out of curiosity, ran the sentiment of the Microtopics, as described above, and found some promisingly suggestive results about the keywords themselves, which will be more thoroughly explored in part two of the dissertation. On a whim I also decided to examine the sentiment of the Microtopics, and found that many of the most controversial were also negative, but this will be explored more in the next two projects of the dissertation.

2.2.2   Discussion

Overall, I found quite consistent results suggesting that scientists Tweet more about a topic when there is more disagreement about that topic (operationalized as negations). There was a significant correlation of .13 between the number of Tweets about a Microtopic and the number of contradictions in those terms. The 25 most talked about were almost half a standard deviation more negated than the average Microtopic, and the 25 most controversial Microtopic were about a third of a standard deviation more than the average Microtopic, and again I found fairly strong evidence at the anecdotal level (e.g., Altmetric top 100s).

All in all, the results suggest that within the context of science, topics and papers that are more discussed (e.g., tweeted) are also more likely to be contradicted. These results have implications for the psychology of science and science evaluation (contradictions are necessary and likely should not be considered bad). Aside from simply the bibliometric functions of Altmetrics, there is great potential to examine Sociological and Psychological questions within the context of science. While the correlations here are smaller than might be imagined, that they are so consistent suggests that more attention might be fruitfully paid to this area. Given that this is the second result suggesting that negations might be good for the amount of discussion and or outcomes, I will now shift the focus toward better identifying cognitive conflict in the topics that scientists study.

2.3 Overall discussion part 2

Overall then, in this first part, I found mixed but promising results, while learning important lessons about the process of doing psychological science on the Internet, especially utilizing text and sentiment analysis tools. I did find, for instance, that papers with comments on them had better outcomes, but I also did not find that the sentiment of those comments actually negative, or that this negativity was related to the outcomes of the paper; though I did find that longer comments were related to better outcomes for the paper and that the more negation terms there are in the text (potentially indicating Controversiality), the more views and media attention the paper receives. In the second study I focused on this Controversiality in particular, finding that the most Tweeted scientific topics also contained more Controversiality than the rest, and that there was a significant positive correlation between the number of Buts and Nots in the tweets and how many Tweets there were.

These results are ok, certainly, not bad, and provide promise both for future studies in these particular areas, e.g., Tweets, Comments, Sentiment, and Controversiality. But more than the mixed results, I learned many lessons during these early studies about how to best operationalize and utilize the data available. Specially, I found that there was often very much fluff in the comments, so while the comment is negative, it is only negative in a single critical sentence, with the rest of the comment buffering or defending this comment. There was also a lack of comments in general and the varying lengths made it difficult, which hindered the analysis, though I did find that this was significantly related to the outcomes. The Tweets were better in that there were more of them and they were of a standardized length (maximum 140 characters), but still there was the fluff problem, and the variability in the way people express things. The Microtopic labels provided an interesting metric, because they are relatively pure indicators of what the problem is the scientists are working on. Looking at Tables 6 and 7 in section 2.2, it is apparent that many of the most discussed and controversial labels carry obvious negative sentiment (e.g., obesity, cancer, stress, extinction); thus, the next projects will examine more in depth these keywords, to see if they are mostly about negative or threatening stimuli. This general analysis is carried out first on the keywords of the PLoS 2014 papers across all areas of science, and then more in depth on a separate set of psychological papers across all publishers, from the year 2013.

Finally, the next set of hypotheses is not as exploratory, and the tests are specific and theory driven, returning simple to interpret evidence for a large and consistent effect that is falsifiable and controversial in the sense that other conclusions could be derived (e.g., many scientists try to avoid controversy, or people want to focus on the good rather than the bad). The same essential results are demonstrated both in one publisher across all areas of science, and then one area of science across all publishers, suggesting a robustness of the effect.

3.0   Cognitive conflict in what scientists study

Having found some evidence that scientists do discuss more when they disagree more, but not really that they talk about more negative things, I next focused on examining whether cognitive conflict also plays a role in the topics that scientists decide to study in the first place. Such an approach allows me to more formally examine Festinger's (1950) second hypothesis, that group members will discuss topics especially when they threaten or are relevant for the well-being of the group; where the goal is to provide hard empirical data about this within the context of scientific debate, also lending evidence for e.g., Kuhn (1962).

These ideas are investigated in two projects, both examining the keywords used to determine what scientists are studying. One study examined the 927,406 individual keywords in the PLoS papers, thus being a single publisher across many disciplines. The other study empiricizes Seligman and Csikszentmihalyi (2014) by studying all 292,790 keywords about psychological papers published in 2013. In general I found that there are more negative than positive keywords and that these negative keywords were studied more often than average.

3.1 Keywords across the scientific enterprise.

The first study I conducted examined the keywords on those papers PLoS published during 2014. This basically allowed me to examine the 'problems' that scientists worked on, by utilizing the keywords of the paper, rather than the texts of or about the paper, which had problems in terms of differing length and fluff, designed to sell or spin as positive the results (Holtz, Deutschmann, Dobewall, 2017). The keywords of a paper offer a more concrete and direct examination of what the paper is about. By utilizing the keywords and counting how often it is used, I can estimate whether scientists study more good or bad keywords, and whether they study those negative keywords more, equal to, or less than the positive and neutral keywords. Particularly the focus will be on whether the sentiment analyzers identify more of these keywords as positive or negative, and how often the keywords are utilized, based on their sentimental content. Again all of the analyses were completed in R and have been presented at the 4th Altmetric Conference in Toronto, Canada, on September 28th, 2017.

3.1.1 Methodological overview and main results

The first sample again consisted of 32,870 scientific articles in all field published in 2014 by the journal PLoS ONE. The data were collected from Almetric.com, and included the title, abstracts, authors, keywords, citations, journals and links of the articles. For this analysis I utilized the keywords that are assigned to the papers by the users of Figshare. Each paper had at least one keyword, with an average of 15.66 keywords without splitting them by space (e.g., cancerous tumor) and a maximum of 63 keywords on a paper. The analysis process consisted of creating a document term matrix, treating the vector of keywords as a comment or tweet in the first projects. The computer then essentially splits the list of keywords into single word units, and counted how many times each unique keyword occurred. One thing to note in the splitting and counting of keywords is that multiple word keywords like 'sexual intercourse' and 'Nervous system physiology' are split, while keywords like 'non-clinical' are not split, as they are one contiguous word. By then taking the sum of each column in the data, the total frequency of usage for each keyword was obtained.

In total there were 927,406 individual keywords in the dataset, with 47,416 unique keywords (including words like 'and'). The average keyword was used 19.56 times with a *SD* of 220.72. The distribution of keywords is positively skewed, with a statistic of 42.28, and it is even more lepto kurtotic, with a statistic of 2,589.49. More than half of the keywords are utilized only once in the dataset, while the maximum number of uses of a single keyword being 18,589, on the keyword 'Biology'. That I split the keywords by spaces is important because it can be seen then just how often the term 'depression' is mentioned, whereas if I didn't split the keywords, how studied depression is would actually be split into e.g., depression scale, depression treatment, depression symptoms. It is also part of the desire to examine how often people mention e.g., symptoms, treatment, and scale.

The top 25 keywords across fields

The top 25 most utilized keywords in all fields during are in Table 8, the entire list of frequencies can be seen at osf.io/. The 25 keywords in the list comprise 19.87% of the overall keywords in the dataset, being utilized 184,290 times in those papers published during 2014 by PLoS. This Top 25 list represents the macro focus of science, and even without the sentiment analysis tools, one sees interesting trends, with 'diseases' taking the 6th spot, 'clinical' taking the 9th spot, 'medicine' taking the 13th spot and 'cancer' taking the 14th spot. None of the terms can really be considered positive, and even when they are neutral, they are still the major problems the scientific enterprise is dealing with. As was mentioned above, even when researchers study something like Biology, there is still the conflict with and desire to remove uncertainty, which itself is negative. These are the topics science is studying in the whole. One other thing to note here is that the document term matrix splits the terms if they are at all different; this is obvious in the case of diseases (6th place) and disease (25th place), incidentally, if we combine these two, disease rises to the fourth spot overall with 13,236 uses; only Biology, And, and Cell are utilized more. In order to get both a more nuanced and standardized understanding of the data, I next sentiment analyzed the keywords.

Sentiment analyzing the keywords

Having examined the most popular keywords and found that some were colloquially negative, I wanted to get a more nuanced and standardized understanding of the sentiment in the keyword. In order to do so I ran the keywords through two well-known sentiment analysis tools; the Hu and Liu (2004) sentiment analyzer and the Sentistrength tool developed by Thelwall, Buckley, Paltoglou, Cai, and Kappas (2010). Both tools are cited more than 500 times and utilize the dictionary approach, essentially comparing whether each keyword has been previously identified as a positive or negative word through various means of testing, such as having people brain storm category terms, comparing their usage in annotated texts, and being checked by experts. The Hu and Liu (2004) analyzer basically identifies whether the keyword is positive, negative, or neutral, with only a single level of intensity for each sentiment. Sentistrength has a more nuanced dictionary, assigning between -5 and +5, also assigning both a positive and negative score for each sentence (in this case keyword). Before analyzing the actual keywords it is interesting to note that both Hu and Liu and Sentistrength have more negative terms in their dictionaries than positive keywords. These biases are displayed in Table 9, providing some early evidence for negativity biases in Linguistics.

Table 8

The Top 25 Most Utilized Keywords Across Science

Keyword	Popularity	Hu & Liu 2004	SentiStrength
biology	18,589	0	0
and	16,776	0	0
cell	14,843	0	0
health	9,155	0	0
genetics	9,019	0	0
diseases	**8,790**	**0**	**-2**
molecular	7,669	0	0
cells	7,231	0	0
clinical	6,767	0	0
ecology	6,605	0	0
research	6,213	0	0
animal	5,970	0	0
medicine	5,941	0	0
cancer	**5,764**	**-1**	**-3**
epidemiology	5,723	0	0
gene	5,712	0	0
analysis	5,549	0	0
biochemistry	5,127	0	0
microbiology	4,966	0	0
physiology	4,945	0	0
system	4,758	0	0
expression	4,635	0	0
plant	4,623	0	0
neuroscience	4,474	0	0
disease	**4,446**	**0**	**-2**

Note. Most sutilized keywords with their sentiment scores in the two columns to the right. Note the bolded showing that Sentistrength (correctly) identifies also disease and diseases.

What is the sentiment of the keywords?

Having sentiment analyzed the keywords, it can be seen how many terms are considered to have a positive or negative sentiment within the context of science. The first thing is that 97% of the keywords were not identified as containing a sentiment, or they were neutral. But of those 3% (or 1,248 keywords) that were identified by Hu and Liu (2004) as having a keyword, 66% of them were negatively valenced (first row Table 10). Also in the table is the overall mean, and a statistical test from 0 demonstrating that this overall mean is significantly different from 0. The Sentistrength analyzer also returns a significant negative overall average, suggesting that both sentiment analyzers identify more negative keywords than positive. While the means are very close to 0, at -.008 and -.022 both are significantly different from 0 with t values below -10. It is interesting to note that Sentistrength identifies more sentiment laden keywords, and has more negative overall averages with 'more significant' results. If instead of taking the overall average, I look only at the top 100 or top 25 most utilized keywords, the results become more negative, where at 100 the mean is -.03, and for the top 25 -.04, though I lose power on the test.

Table 9

Number of Words in Each of the Sentiment Dictionaries

	-5	-4	-3	-2	-1	0	1	2	3	4	5	Total
Hu Liu					4,783	Na	2,006					6,789
Sentistrength	8	132	340	1440	52	Na	179	238	128	26	4	2,547
%s	-5	-4	-3	-2	-1	0	1	2	3	4	5	
Hu Liu					70	Na	30					100%
Sentistrength	0	05	13	57	02	Na	07	09	05	01	0	100%

Note. Below is also the percentage of the total keywords in each sentiment category (to make most clear the biases).

Interestingly, the two sentiment scores are only correlated at .44, though this might also be because there is a low granularity in the Hu and Liu analyzer. No matter which results one interprets, they consistently suggest that overall there are more negative keywords than positive or neutral ones. Here one can see some of the first empirical evidence that scientists study more negative keywords, in sheer number, than positive keywords. At a minimum it is evidence for Schwarz's (1989) hypothesis about people speaking in more detail about negative topics, though I would more generally suggest that it is evidence that science is a problem solving enterprise, and that scientists are biased toward solving problems and negative things with their science.

Table 10

Number of Words in Each Category Per Sentiment Analyzer and the Average Overall

	-4	-3	-2	-1	0	1	2	3	4	nwords	Mean	Se	t
1.				822	46,167	426				47,416	-0.008	0.00	-11.24
2.	0	48	171	928	45,978	218	64	7	1	47,416	-0.022	0.00	-20.56

	-4	-3	-2	-1	0	1	2	3	4	nwords	Mean	Se	t
1.				65.9%		34.1%				1,248	-.317	.03	-11.82
2.	0%	3.34%	11.9%	64.58%		15.17%	4.45%	0.49%	0.07%	1,437	-.726	.03	-24.31

Note. The top table has the raw number of words in each dictionary, with the overall average and *t* test. The bottom table removes the neutral keywords and presents the percentages in each dictionary, the overall mean, and a t test on the average compared to 0.

Top 25 most studied keywords containing a sentiment

Looking back on Table 8, you can see that most of the most utilized keywords are neutral, with only a few being identified as being negative. In order to get a better idea of the keywords the sentiment analyzers are identifying, I compiled the 25 most utilized keywords that were tagged by either analyzer as having a sentiment (Table 11). The most striking thing about the table is that nearly all of the keywords are negative, with 23 of the 25 being negatively valenced. Even the words that are tagged as positive, 'care' (pos. 5) and 'dynamics' (pos. 13), are not really positive, as care is most often paired with 'health care', 'critical care' or 'quality of care' and even then generally associated with how to improve it (indicating a lack of it). Again we see that the analyzers dissociated 'disease' (pos. 3) and diseases (pos. 1), cancer (pos. 2) and cancers (pos. 6), and infection (pos. 9) and infections (pos. 11). Still all three pairs of terms are in the top 25 utilizes keywords with a sentiment and utilized more than 500 times each. Note also that the keywords rat (pos. 21) and regression (pos. 17) are in the top 25 keywords, and should probably be considered false positives / negatives. One can separately ask if our negative thoughts about rats influenced our decision to make them the subjects of all the horrid scientific experimentation we are uncomfortable doing to other humans, or whether statistians or researchers might intentionally name their fields of study negatively, as negative things appear to get more attention (Festinger, 1954).

Are negative concepts studied more than positive concepts?

Having found that there are more unique negative keywords in the dataset, and that many of the most studied keywords with a sentiment were negative, I wanted to next examine whether the negative keywords are studied more, on average, across the entire dataset. Table 12 contains the average number of times each keyword was used across each sentiment group, across the two sentiment analyzers. The results of an ANOVA (treating each sentiment group as its own group) and a regression (treating sentiment as a linear score) are on the right of Table 12. What can be seen is that the negative keywords are utilized more than both the positive and the neutral keywords. The Hu and Liu results are not as convincing, in either the ANOVA or regression results, as the Sentistrength results are stronger, but are still significant and in the expected directions, and it can be clearly seen in the means of the groups. It should also be noted that there are more negative keywords than positive keywords. This is important as if there is no effect, we would expect larger random samples to be closer to the grand mean (while in the data the more accurate estimations are farther from the overall mean).

Table 11

The Top 25 Most Utilized Sentiment Laden Keywords

	Keyword	Popularity	Hu & Liu	SentiStrength	Average Score
1	diseases	8,790	0	-2	-1
2	cancer	5,764	-1	-3	-2
3	disease	4,446	0	-2	-1
4	infectious	4,137	0	-1	-0.5
5	care	3,001	0	1	0.5
6	cancers	2,019	0	-3	-1.5
7	disorders	1,829	0	-1	-0.5
8	risk	1,439	-1	-1	-1
9	infection	1,419	-1	-1	-1
10	stress	1,272	-1	-1	-1
11	infections	1,115	-1	-1	-1
12	virus	791	-1	0	-0.5
13	dynamics	737	0	1	0.5
14	inflammation	643	-1	0	-0.5
15	nervous	640	-1	-2	-1.5
16	death	619	-1	-2	-1.5
17	regression	537	-1	-1	-1
18	invasive	509	-1	0	-0.5
19	resistance	494	-1	0	-0.5
20	obesity	472	0	-1	-0.5
21	rat	469	0	-1	-0.5
22	critical	466	-1	-1	-1
23	chronic	438	-1	-2	-1.5
24	parasitic	437	0	-2	-1
25	emergency	419	-1	-1	-1

Note. The keywords are from those papers published by PLoS in 2014. Note how the sentiment analyzers don't always agree, and that the Sentistrength in general provides better coverage.

If I treat the sentiment groups as a linear scale, I can run a regression on the number of uses as a function of the keyword's sentiment (Table 5, right side). The Hu and Lui (2004) analyzer's three categories suggest that for each group the keyword traverses (from negative, to neutral, to positive) results in, on average, 13 less uses; this is significant with a *t* value of 2.15 and a *p* value of .03. Once again the newer, more nuanced, Sentistrength analyzer has better results where traversing from each sentiment group from -5 to +5 would result in on average 24.79 less uses as one moves from more negative toward more positive keyword groupings. Remember that most of the keywords are neutral, with even only 7 keywords in the +3 keyword grouping and only 1 keyword in the +4 keyword group (Table 12).

Table 12

Means per sentiment group, ANOVA, and Regression results.

Descriptives									ANOVA		Regression			
-4	-3	-2	-1	0	1	2	3	4	F	p	B	SE	t	p
Hu			37.43	19.31	14.72				4.61	.04	-13.45	6.26	-2.15	0.03
Sen na	188.85	104.31	30.79	18.82	27.61	8.91	1.71	1	32.45	>.01	-24.79	4.35	-5.7	0

Note: Average raw usage for each sentiment group, SEs and overall means can be computed utilizing the ns in Table 3 N = 47,415. The overall average was 19.56, across all keywords.

3.1.2 Discussion

No matter how I looked at the keywords, there was evidence for the hypothesized negativity bias; lending support to the hypothesis or suggestion that (some form of) cognitive conflict plays a role when scientists decide what they will work on. There were more unique negative terms overall, lending support for Schwarz's (1989) suggestion that people would talk about negative things in more detail. These negative topics were also more studied on average, lending support for the literature on the negativity bias more generally.

One thing to notice here is that the Hu and Liu (2004) results are notably weaker, in general. This might be due to the lower number of words the Hu and Liu analyzer identifies, or because of the greater granularity of Sentistrength. Regardless, one can easily determine from the top 25 utilized sentiment terms (Table 11) that Sentistrength identifies the terms more accurately and completely, with Hu and Liu (2004) not identifying plurals (e.g., Diseases, Cancers, and Infections) but also not identifying Disease in the first place.

Having found these exciting and promising results in the original dataset, the next step is to show the same result again with a different set of data. Whereas in the original dataset we looked at papers published across all fields by a single publisher, PLoS, the next step was to look only within one field, Psychology, across all publishers indexed by the Web of Science.

Testing the ideas specifically within the context of psychology has several benefits including increasing the expertise both the authors and eventual readers have about the keywords, test the ideas in another context, and specifically allowing us to provide (among) the first empirical evidence for Seligman and Csikszentmihalyi's (2014) suggestion that Psychology in particular studies too many negative things, though I will argue with them that this is not a problem to be fixed but an essential part of our psychology and the purpose of the scientific enterprise, in general.

3.2 Evidence for a negativity bias in psychological science.

Having found quite promising results utilizing the keywords on papers to examine whether negative topics are more numerous and often studied, I next decided to replicate this idea on another dataset, trying again to fix some of the potential problems with the last study. One of the limitations was that I was only looking at one publisher, rather than at an area of science; thus I decided to examine across all publishers within a single area of study, Psychology. This move also has the advantages of coming closer to our own expertise, and empiricizing Seligman and Csikszentmihalyi's (2014) suggestion that Psychology has become too negative. Another way I improved the study was to again utilize the LIWC analyzer, as in the first study. The study is also interesting because demonstrating the biases among psychological scientists drives home the power and fundamental nature of the biases. Thus, I ask, within Psychology, whether more unique negatively valenced keywords are utilized, and whether the negative keywords identified would be utilized more than the positively and neutrally valenced keywords. I finally demonstrated the effect in the context of emotion studies, showing that there are more negative emotions and that they are studied more.

3.2.1 Methodological overview and main results.
The starting dataset is all those 23,394 papers published at Web of Science between January and October (23rd) 2013 that utilize Psychology as a category label. The data came from the Web of Science, which were manually pulled for another, previous, project (Buttliere, 2013), and are not only available and familiar but quite comprehensive, including the title, abstracts, authors, the journal, and many other metrics besides. The data I was particularly interested in here are the columns of keywords available about the papers; one is author assigned keywords and another were harvested automatically from the titles and cited papers (Web of Knowledge, 2017). Metadata documentation is a little bit unclear for the variables, but one of the variables has no keywords for 4,506 of the papers and only an average of 3.4 keywords per paper, while the other variable misses keywords for only 955 of the papers, and an average of 8.06 keywords and a standard deviation of 2.85 per paper and a maximum of 10 keywords per paper. Nine records were removed for incorrect formatting.

Having the lists of keywords, I was then able to utilize the 'text mining' package in R, in order clean the texts, identify unique keywords, and count how often the keywords were utilized. There are several advantages to utilizing this process, the largest one being that it splits the keywords by all hyphens and spaces, removes punctuation, and generally does a good job of best identifying the individual keywords. An example of this is that if I analyze without splitting by e.g., the spaces, 'single' keywords such as "depression symptoms" or "depression scale" would be considered two individual keywords, and I would miss that actually both keywords or papers are about depression. Splitting by the space leaves us with 292,790 truly individual keywords on the 23,385 papers, with 12,241 unique keywords across the papers. These keywords are utilized, on average, 23.92 times. There are many different decisions to be made at these initial steps of the analysis (e.g., to split the data or not), and while these small changes do not change the substantial outcomes of the study, but I made the full analysis script and materials available at osf.io/ rjavn/, so you can explore on your own. Having counted the most utilized keywords I begin the substantial examination.

The top 25 keywords in the field

The top 25 most utilized keywords in Psychological Science during 2013 are in Table 13, the entire list of keywords with their frequencies is available at osf.io/rjavn/. While the dataset is large (12,241 unique keywords), the fact that disorder (pos. 6) and disorders (pos. 10) is split still demonstrates the potential for keywords to be split by small differences. The 25 keywords in Table 13 make up 14.58% of all the 292,790 individual keywords used in the data frame, being utilized 42,685 times.

A cursory look at Table 13 (maybe cover the right columns first) suggests that none of the top keywords should really be considered positive, while at least disorder(s), risk, depression, stress, and anxiety should probably be considered negative. It is interesting that if one combines 'disorder' and 'disorders', they become the most popular keyword, being then utilized 4,048 times (disorder should probably be considered negative). These results provide a first indication that Seligman Seligman and Csikszentmihalyi (2014) were correct in their assertion that psychology very often studies the negative or wrong rather than the right.

More than these few easily identifiable negative keywords and corresponding lack of positive keywords, I would like to standardize and empiricize that the result goes beyond just those top 25 most utilized keywords. Thus, I submitted the keywords to sentiment analyzers, utilizing the expertise of several groups of linguists, to determine the positivity or negativity of the topics psychologists study.

Table 13

The Top 25 Most Utilized Keywords

	Keyword	Popularity	score.score	Sentiment.Liwc	SentiStrengthOverall
1	behavior	3,315	0	0	0
2	children	2,412	0	0	0
3	memory	2,375	0	0	0
4	self	2,326	0	0	0
5	model	2,213	0	0	0
6	disorder	2,169	-1	0	-1
7	health	2,068	0	0	0
8	performance	1,926	0	0	0
9	social	1,880	0	0	0
10	disorders	1,852	0	0	-1
11	differences	1,675	0	0	0
12	risk	1,512	-1	-1	-1
13	depression	1,472	-1	-1	-3
14	cortex	1,461	0	0	0
15	attention	1,454	0	0	0
16	stress	1,451	-1	-1	-1
17	life	1,375	0	0	0
18	scale	1,287	0	0	0
19	brain	1,274	0	0	0
20	use	1,237	0	0	0
21	cognitive	1,236	0	0	0
22	mental	1,197	0	0	0
23	personality	1,193	0	0	0
24	anxiety	1,171	-1	-1	-2
25	adolescents	1,154	0	0	0
Total and averages		42,685	-0.2	-0.16	-0.36

Note. Across those 23,303 psychological papers published during 2013, with their sentiment. I suggest covering the sentiment scores before reading the list.

Systematizing the analysis.

While one can colloquially agree that several of the top keywords/ topics psychologists study are clearly negative (at least disorder, risk, depression, stress, and anxiety) and that none clearly positive keywords, this is not really empirical evidence. To formalize the analysis I compared the keywords to several well tested and utilized sentiment analyzers. This also opens up new questions, such as whether there are more positive or negative words overall, and whether the positive words or the negative words are utilized on average differently.

The sentiment analyzers

In order to systematize the understanding of the sentiment in the keywords, I utilized three of the best standardized and most trusted sentiment analyzers around, the Hu and Liu (2004) dictionaries, the Linguistic Inquiry and Word Count tool from Pennebaker et al. (2015), and Sentistrength from Thelwall, et al. (2010). Each citation analysis tool is cited more than 500 times, with Hu and Liu and LIWC being cited more than 2,000 times. All three are clear and easy to understand, essentially utilizing different versions of the dictionary approach. There are reasons for choosing these particular sentiment analyzers, including that Hu and Liu (2004) is one of the original sentiment analysis dictionaries, LIWC is essentially the psychological standand, and Sentistrength is developed by a bibliometrician (and so has been used in bibliometric analyses). They all utilize a general dictionary approach, where the computer compares the words to a dictionary, but they handle this data in different ways (for more detail see Buttliere & Buder, in prep). Fortunately because the 'texts' are only single words, these differences do not really affect the analysis, and thus the major differences are in the dictionaries each analyzer uses.

It is interesting to note that all three of these well standardized sentiment analysis tools have more negative words in their dictionaries than positive words (Table 14). LIWC has the most equal dictionaries, with 42% positive terms, while Hiu and Liu has 30% positive terms and Sentistrength has only 22% positive terms. That each of these dictionaries has more negative terms does support the notion that humans discuss more specifically when discussing negative things (Schwarz, 1989). Despite these biases that are normal in their own communities, much more work has been put into standardizing these dictionaries than could or would functionally be put into sorting out the positivity or negativity of the keywords on their own, and I consider it as evidence for the negativity bias in language or at least the more generally, rather than just in Psychology.

Table 14

Number of Words in Each of the Sentiment Dictionaries

	-5	-4	-3	-2	-1	0	1	2	3	4	5	Total
1. Hu					4,783		2,006					6,789
2. LIWC					744		620					1,364
3. Senti	8	132	340	1440	52		179	238	128	26	4	2,547
	-5	-4	-3	-2	-1	0	1	2	3	4	5	
1.					70%		30%					
2.					58%		42%					
3.	0%	05%	13%	57%	02%		07%	09%	05%	01%	0%	

Note. Below is also the percentage of the total keywords in each sentiment category (to make clear the biases).

What is the sentiment of the keywords overall?

The first question I wanted to examine with the sentiment data was whether there are more positive or more negative unique keywords in the dataset overall (and thus what the average of the sentiment is). This is simply a matter of counting the number of words that matched each dictionary, and then examining whether the mean is different from 0 for the overall dataset.

All three of the sentiment analyzers return an overall average that is negative and statistically different from 0 (Table 15). The Hu and Liu dictionaries found 743 negative words and 366 positive keywords in the list of 12,241 keywords; indicating that two of every three sentiment laden keywords was negative. The overall 'average sentiment' of the keywords was -.031 [-0.036: -0.025], $t = -11.38$, p very far below (<<) .01. While the overall sentiment is very close to 0 at -.03, 11,132 (or 91%) of the keywords were neutral; so it could not be far from 0 no matter what. Looking more closely at the top 100 gives a mean of -.04, and the top 25 gives a mean of -.20, indicating that 20% of the top 25 keywords are negative. These results are a first indication that as one moves toward more popular keywords, there are more negative keywords, and indeed, even the mean of the top 25 is statistically different

from 0 (M = -.20, SE = .08, t = -2.44, p = .02). This is a small and underpowered test, but

remember that these are then the 25 most studied topics in Psychology; that there is such a

strong negative effect is important and shows how powerful the effect is. The LIWC results

are largely the same, identifying 284 negative keywords and 295 positive keywords, with an

overall average of -.01 [-.011: -.003], t = -3.41, p = .00063. Again, the average for the top 100

is more negative, at -.03 (with a t of -1), and an average for the top 25 of -.16, again being

significant t = -2.14, p = .04. Sentistrength is again the same, identifying 883 negative words

and 211 positive words, with an overall average of -.08 [-.08: -.06], for a t value of -19.31.

Again the averages for the top 100 and top 25 were consecutively higher, with averages of

-.16 (t = -2.47) and -.36 (t = -2.37, p = .03). Note that Sentistrength identifies the most

sentiment laden words and has the furthest average value of the three sentiment analyzers. It

thus appears that there is a negativity bias in the keywords, such that psychologists study

more unique negatively valenced keywords than positively valenced keywords, and that these

biases become stronger as one looks at the more utilized keywords.

Table 15

Number of Words in Each Category Per Sentiment Analyzer and the Average Overall.

	-3	-2	-1	0	1	2	3	Total	Average	t value	P value
1.			743	11,132	366			1109	-0.03	-11.38	>.01
2.			384	11,562	295			679	-0.01	-3.42	>.01
3.	65	186	634	11,145	154	51	6	1096	-0.08	-19.31	>.01

	-3	-2	-1	0	1	2	3	Total	%Neutral
1.	0	0	0.67		0.33	0	0	1	91
2.	0	0	0.57		0.43	0	0	1	94
3.	0.06	0.17	0.58		0.14	0.05	0.01	1.01	91

Note. Below that is the percentages of positive and negative keywords. The sample size for all
three analyzers is 12,241 keywords.

Thus, the results first suggest that there are more unique negative keywords than

positive or neutral keywords in the data. While this is impressive, one could argue that this is actually the result of the dictionaries utilized, and indeed the biases in the database follow quite closely with the overall biases in the dictionaries (comparing Tables 14 and 15). Still the fact that there are more negative keywords toward the most utilized keywords is an indicator, and in fact it has been suggested that positive keywords are utilized more often (Boucher & Osgood, 1969), even within academic and psychological texts (Holtz et al., 2017). One difference between these texts and our own is that they look at full texts, rather than the keywords of the texts. Another potentially important difference is that thus far I have not looked at the frequency of the terms, rather than just how many unique terms there are. In order to remove this potential problem (though as stated the inequalities in the dictionaries themselves should indicate something), I next examined how often the positive and negative keywords were utilized on average, expecting negative keywords to be utilized more, despite research suggesting that positive words are utilized more often (Boucher & Osgood, 1969).

Are negative concepts studied more than positive or neutral concepts?

I found that there were more unique negative topics studied than positive topics, but this did not actually answer whether the topics were studied more. Indeed, it could very well be that the positive keywords, even though there are statistically less of them, are utilized more; Garcia, Garas & Schweitzer (2012) for instance suggested that negative words are utilized more specifically, while positive words are used in more general contexts. Thus, here I treated each sentiment category as a group and examined whether the positive and negative terms are utilized differently, on average.

In order to test whether the negative keywords were utilized more than the positive or neutral keywords, I examined whether those negative keywords were mentioned more often, on average. The average keyword, overall, was utilized 23.92 times, with an SD of 107.09 (remember the maximum is 3,315 uses), positively skewed, and mesokurtic. Thus, while Table 16 indicates the raw average number of times each sentiment keyword group was utilized, to aid interpretation, for the statistics, I utilized a logged and standardized version of the data. When examining the sentiment groups as different units or as a linear factor the results are the same, there are statistical differences in the groups in terms of how often the keywords are utilized, and there is a negative linear relation between the sentiment of the keyword and how often it is utilized (Table 16). These results are particularly surprising given that the groups of negative words are consistently larger than the positive keyword groups and if there were nothing going on here, we would expect for the larger groups to be closer to the mean (Galton, 1889).

Table 16

Average, Raw, Usage for Each Sentiment Group

	-3	-2	-1	0	1	2	3	ANOVA	B	SE	F	P
1.			35.37	23.21	22.24			9.53	-0.09	0.03	-3.09	<.001
2.			43.57	23.22	25.55			6.72	-0.09	-0.04	-2.60	<.01
3.	79.42	34.91	32.55	22.88	28.99	18.39	22.17	27.68	-0.11	-0.02	-5.26	<.001

Note. Raw usage and a statistical test treating the groups as independent and as a linear factor. N = 12,241.

More advanced analysis, gives a more nuanced answer, though (Table 17). If we treat the group of negative keywords as a baseline and compare whether the neutral and positive groups are statistically different from it, the neutral keywords are always utilized statistically less, but the positive keywords are not utilized statistically less in the Hu and Liu analyzer, and only marginally significantly less in the LIWC analyzer. The Sentistrength analyzer does show that the keywords are utilized significantly less all the way up until the most positive keywords, which are not significantly different from the most negativity utilized keywords. One thing to keep in mind, especially about this last result is that there are actually only 6 keywords in the group, so in some ways finding a statistical difference is difficult. In all three cases though, it is clear that the negative keywords are at least a quarter of a standard deviation above the mean.

Table 17

Regression, Treating the Negatively Sentimented Keywords as the Baseline

1. Hu & Liu	Beta	*SE*	*t* value	*p* value	
(Intercept)	0.25	0.04	6.74	.00	***
Neutral	-0.27	0.04	-7.16	.00	***
Positive	-0.03	0.06	-0.40	.70	
AIC: 34676					
2. LIWC	Beta	*SE*	*t* value	*p* value	
(Intercept)	0.32	0.05	6.22	.00	***
Neutral	-0.33	0.05	-6.41	.00	***
Positive	-0.13	0.08	-1.72	.08	.
AIC: 34694					
3. Sentistrength	Beta	*SE*	*t* value	*p* value	
(Intercept)	0.57	0.12	4.62	.00	***
Negative -2	-0.38	0.14	-2.65	.01	**
Negative -1	-0.40	0.13	-3.10	.00	**
Neutral	-0.59	0.12	-4.76	.00	***
Positive 1	-0.43	0.15	-2.90	.00	**
Positive 2	-0.47	0.19	-2.51	.01	*
Positive 3	-0.31	0.43	-0.73	.47	
AIC: 34699					

Note. ***$p < .001$, **$p < .01$. *Note that the results suggest that the positive are not significantly less in the Hu and Liu analyzer, it becomes so in the more recent and accurage sentiment analyzers.*

3.2.2 Demonstrating a negativity bias within Emotion Science

The final way I will demonstrate that negativity bias is within the minds of

psychological scientists is to examine specifically emotion research, to see if psychologists

study more negative or positive emotions. There are several reasons for making this final step.

One is that I expect it to be among the clearest demonstrations possible, given that fear was

one of the first emotions studied and that it was the first to be understood physiologically.

Another reason is that some of our colleagues believe most of the above results are driven

mostly by Clinical Psychology, which largely focuses on fixing disorders and other

discomforts; of course they never explain why Clinical Psychology is the largest field in the first place, or admit that this in itself could be driven by the negativity bias I am trying to demonstrate here. In any case, by focusing on the emotions theorists posit as basic, we should be removing any effect of clinical psychology in any case.

The analysis will largely follow the outline from above, utilizing as the sample those emotions which have been named by the 14 theories of basic emotion Ortony and Turner (1990) outlined in their Psychological Review paper. I expected to find that most of the 'basic' emotions are negative in sentiment, and that the negative basic emotions will be studied more than the positive basic emotions. At the end I examined which is a better predictor of the number of times the emotion is studied, how often it is mentioned as basic by theorists, or its sentiment.

Simply looking over Table 18 already suggests that many emotional theorists posit more different basic negative emotions than basic positive emotions. For instance, of Ekman et al.'s 6 basic emotions, Anger, Disgust, Fear, and Sadness are all negative, while Happiness and Surprise are positive, though an argument could be made that surprise is also negative (the first instinct is to retreat). William James suggests four basic emotions, those being Fear, Grief, Rage, and Joy, while John Watson posited Fear, Rage, and Love. Negativity bias.

There were 35 unique emotion terms utilized; the most commonly mentioned among them were: Fear (mentioned 9 times), Anger (7 times), Disgust (6 times), Sadness (5 times), Surprise (5 times), and then Happiness in 6th place, being mentioned only 4 times. These results are especially surprising as the Pollyanna research suggests we use the positive terms more often and in broader contexts and one might expect the concentration to lead to more mentions of e.g., Happiness; driving home the results quite well in my opinion. If I take the overall sentiment of these 35 keywords, I found an average of -.37 [-.64, -.09], with a t value of -2.72 and a p of .01, despite the small sample size.

Table 18

14 Theories of the Basic Emotions and the Emotions They Suggest. Note the negativity.

Theorist	Basic Emotions
Plutchik	Acceptance, anger, anticipation, disgust, joy, fear, sadness, surprise
Arnold	Anger, aversion, courage, dejection, desire, despair, fear, hate, Hope, love, sadness
Ekman, Friesen, and Ellsworth	Anger, disgust, fear, happiness, sadness, surprise
Frijda	Desire, happiness, interest, surprise, wonder, sorrow
Gray	Rage, terror, anxiety, joy
Izard	Anger, contempt, disgust, distress, fear, guilt, interest, joy, shame, surprise
James, W.	Fear, grief, love, rage
McDougall	Anger, disgust, elation, fear, subjection, tender-emotion, wonder
Mowrer	Pain, pleasure
Oatley and Johnson-Laird	Anger, disgust, anxiety, happiness, sadness
Panksepp	Expectancy, fear, rage, panic
Tomkins	Anger, interest, contempt, disgust, distress, fear, joy, shame, surprise
Watson	Fear, love, rage
Weiner and Graham	Happiness, sadness

Note: Table is from Ortony and Turner (1990) and lists 14 theories of the basic emotions.

The next step in the analysis is to examine how often each of these proposed basic emotions are utilized as keywords in the sample of papers. Table 19 contains the top 10 keywords, listed in order of their popularity, and their sentiment from the three analyzers. The SentiStrenth score has been changed to a -1, 0, or 1, simply to ease interpretation of the metric. The negativity bias is well demonstrated here, with only two of the top ten keywords being positive, and only 1, happiness, being utilized more than 100 times. Anxiety, Distress, Pain, Fear, Anger, and Panic are all studied more than Happiness, providing evidence for Seligman and Csikszentmihalyi's (2014) assertion that Psychology is negatively biased.

A final interesting analysis that having the data from the theorists allows is to compare whether the sentiment of the keyword or how often it has been mentioned by theorists better predicts how often it is utilized. Utilizing Kendal Rank Correlations as displayed in Table 20, you can see that how often an emotion is mentioned by theorists is not really related to how often it is used as a keyword ($r = .03$). Conversely, the sentiment of the keyword is related at $r = -.33$ to how often it is utilized as a keyword, suggesting that as a keyword becomes more negative, it also becomes more utilized. These results, that the sentiment of the keyword is a better predictor of how much it is studied than how many emotion theorists agree it is basic, suggest that studying emotions is not purely about understanding them, but that there are other factors, and that especially that the sentiment of the keyword is a better predictor of how often it is studied than how often it is mentioned as basic by theorists.

Table19

The Top 10 Studied 'Basic' Emotions

Row.names	Keyword	Usage	Frequency	HuLiu	LIWC	SentiStrength	Avg.Sent
1	anxiety	1138	2	-1	-1	-1	-1
2	distress	366	2	-1	-1	-1	-1
3	pain	214	1	-1	-1	-1	-1
4	fear	210	9	-1	-1	-1	-1
5	anger	120	7	-1	-1	-1	-1
6	panic	104	1	-1	-1	-1	-1
7	happiness	101	4	1	1	1	1
8	grief	62	1	-1	-1	-1	-1
9	guilt	62	1	-1	-1	-1	-1
10	love	42	3	1	1	1	1

Note. Ranked by how often they were studied, also with how often they are mentioned by the theorists and their sentiments.

Table 20

Correlations

	Frequency	Popularity	Avg.Sent
Frequency	1	0.03	-0.07
Popularity	0.03	1	-0.33
Avg.Sent	-0.07	-0.33	1

Note. How often emotions are mentioned as basic, how often it is studied mentioned as a keyword, and its average sentiment from the three analyzers.

3.2.3 Discussion

The results from the analysis of the negativity bias among psychological science was as or more successful than the analysis in the PLoS data. More unique negative keywords were studied than positive keywords, and more papers were written about negative topics than neutral or (slightly) positive keywords. More than this, I found that these results were particularly clear and demonstrable with emotion research, showing that both the top most consistently mentioned and studied 'basic' emotions are actually negative. Finally, I showed that the amount of research about an emotion was better predicted by its sentiment than how often it is cited as 'basic' by theorists (i.e., how important it is thought to be in our psychology).

3.3 Overall discussion part 3

Overall these results, paired with the results from the PLoS analysis, suggest that there is a reasonably reliable negativity bias in the keywords scientists utilize to describe their papers. This finding provides among the first evidence for several previously mentioned propsitions, including: Festinger's (1950) hypothesis that people and groups will discuss more those stimuli that are threatening, Seligman and Csikszentmihalyi's (2014) assertion that psychology specifically has a negativity bias, and the more general assertion that science is a problem solving and uncertainty reducing enterprise (Kuhn, 1962; Popper, 2004). More generally the results also suggest that psychological principles can be applied to better understand how science works, and even things like how scientific attention gets paid to certain topics or problems. These hypotheses were supported both across all fields of science from a single publisher and across all publishers within the specific context of psychology.

4.0 General summary

Calls to improve the scientific enterprise have grown enormously over the last decade, and major changes have come to formal and informal scientific communication. Especially the use of the Internet has changed the way that scientists communicate, both opening up new opportunities to communicate about science, and along with it new ways to study scientific communication (Buttliere, 2014; Priem, Piwowar, & Hemminger, 2012). Utilizing these new data, here I empirically tested a long standing philosophical hypothesis about how science works, or how science *should* work. Rather than focusing on improving how scientists answer their questions (e.g., preregistration, increasing sample sizes), the goal of the dissertation was to start a dissusion on how to improve the questions the scientists ask in the first place, or more generally how scientists come to ask the questions they do in the first place.

The thesis examined the proposition that the things scientists talk about and the topics they study are determined, in part, by cognitive conflict, that being defined as competing ideas in the mind at the same time. Two projects particularly focused on whether scientists would discuss topics more when they disagreed about them more, focusing on the comments on the webpage of the paper and the Tweets about scientific topics. The results were in general promising; finding that papers with (ostansibly negative; Radicchi, 2012) comments, especially those longer comments with more negation terms, do have better outomes in general, and that scientific topics about which more discussions are started on Twitter also contain more negation terms. These studies clearly suggest a positive relationship between the amount of attention paid to a paper or topic and amount of negation or argumentation in that discussion, lending empirical evidence that Festinger's (1950) hypothesis about informal social communication also holds within informal scientific communication.

Having found that scientists were more likely to discuss things they disagreed about more, I also wanted to examine whether scientists were more likely to study things which were negative or threatening to the group's well being (Festinger, 1950). Two additional studies suggested that this is the case, finding that there are more unique negative terms in an absolute sense (so more negative topics are studied than positive topics) and that these unique topics have more papers written about them, on average. These results were consistent both in a dataset examining papers across all fields of science across a single large publisher, and in a dataset containing psychology papers across all publishers. The differences were especially obvious in comparing the most popular keywords, the most popular negative and positive keywords, or if one examined the number of positive and negative 'basic' emotions and how often they are studied. These results provided convincing evidence that scientists pay attention to especially negative topics, and empiricized Seligman and Csikszentmihalyi's (2014) claim that psychology has a negativity bias in it.

4.1 Implications and contributions

The findings of the studies, such as that more discussed topics contain more contradictions in those discussions, or that scientists study more negative topics, more often, have several direct implications, including for how scientists should be thinking the scientific enterprise works. One of the most important contributions and implications is in evidencing that psychological concepts and truths also seem to hold within the context of science. The suggestion is that much more can be applied and learned, both for understanding science in the specific, but also Psychology in the general; testing psychological theories in science is feasible and economical.

That more discussed topics were also disagreed about more, and that threatening topics were studied more than non threatening topics also lends credence to the fact that science is in fact an uncertainty reducing and problem solving enterprise (Maslow, 2004; Popper, 1934/ 2005). Understanding this notion has implications for the very way that science is done and funded. Knowing that other scientists are more likely to talk about things they disagree about, it makes sense for a scientist to take up controversial questions, for, even if others tell them that they are wrong, it is good for them and the field at large, in the long run. Similarly, while traditionally, funding bodies stay away from controversial work, the results suggest that there might even be added value in setting up something like adversarial collaborations, where competing teams struggle against each other in best designing studies to test hypotheses. Another way to encourage this collaborative discourse would be to highlight the fact most or all of the hypotheses about how the most effective science is done include cognitive conflict and discourse (e.g., Socratic Method, Hegelian Dialectic).

Another implication of the work is to demonstrate the far reaching effects of cognitive conflict and dissonance theory more generally throughout our psychology. Our data suggest that while Festinger (1950) was originally simply talking about informal social communication, these same basic hypotheses also apply to both formal and informal communication within the context of science. The far reaching effects of cognitive conflict are outlined in the introduction, but actually having the empirical evidence for these effects drives home how fundamental of the construct is in our psychology and society.

A final implication of the work is that I empiricized Seligman and Csikszentmihalyi (2014) that Psychology is biased toward studying the negative, rather than the positive. The question then becomes whether this is something to fight against, or something that can actually be good. If we follow Seligman and Csikszentmihalyi (2014), we should see this as a problem to be solved. Conversely, if we take the perspective that science is about problem solving, it would make sense to focus on the negative (the problems), in order to identify and fix them. Taking the problem solving perspective on science makes a lot of sense, in my opinion and matches well within the larger frame of dissonance theory and Psychology generally.

4.2 Methodological innovations

More than answer interesting theoretical questions, the goal was also to develop and utilize methodologically innovative techniques for answering the questions. This is most obvious in the data, where I utilized behavioral residue on the Internet to answer the questions, rather than collect survey responses or other experimental data, as most of the previous work on cognitive conflict has done. Not only do these data not have the potential problems that they come from the lab setting and experimentation, collecting new data from scientists is very expensive, not only because they are such a hard population to reach, but when you reach them the demands on their time often mean they have none left for you. Utilizing the behavioral data from the Internet allows us to examine real, raw, uncensored, interactions between scientists, in their natural settings, without making them go out of their way. It is my belief that these behavioral residues contain very much potential, even being the future of psychological enquiry, in general.

Another methodological innovation was to make all of the data and code available online for others to use. Already these data and code are being utilized in other projects, including a project on whether Wikipedia articles on negative topics also receive more attention and edits (Yenikent, Buttliere, Holtz, & Kimmerle, In Preparation), another on whether sentiment changes across abstracts (with authors describing the problem first and the solution of the problem last; Holtz, Buttliere, & Gnambs, In preparation), and finally a project on whether the nouns within scientific abstracts are negative (being the problems), while the verbs are positive (indicating that we are fixing, solving, improving the problems; Buder & Buttliere, In Preparation). The goal of our work is to create a more efficient and effective science, by collaborating to answer more interesting questions in more resource efficient ways.

More generally among philosophers who think about this conflict plays an important role. For instance, in Popper's *Logic of Science* (1934/ 2005) he calls for identifying risky conjectures which can be falsified, and then trying to falsify them (i.e., put holes in your own theory). Kuhn (1962) became famous for his notions of the paradigm, anomalies, and paradigm shifts, defining an anomaly as, "an occurrence or set of occurrences that does not fit existing ways of ordering phenomena" (Kuhn, 1962, p. 120).

4.3 Limitations and future directions

Identifying the important role of cognitive conflict is important, but it is still important to examine where else cognitive conflict reliably shows itself, where it doesn't show itself, and why there are different outcomes. While most of my results were positive, it is still a question as to why longer comments were not more negative, as one might expect from previous literature (Sen & Lerman, 2007), though I did not decide to focus on why this was the case.

Another important area where the field and specifically this work could be improved is in its operationalization of cognitive conflict. One of the most commonly cited problems is the elusive nature of cognitive conflict. Within the context of the thesis, I looked both at arguments between scientists, and at topics which cause scientists and society at large pain. This distinction can be seen especially in the first project, as the amount of negations, rather than the sentiment per se, was related to outcomes; where sentiment is more words like disease, cancer, and infection. These topics certainly indicate one form of cognitive conflict, and it will be an important and beneficial step moving forward for scientists to more clearly delineate whether they are aiming to measure the conflict caused by the topics themselves (e.g., cancer), or the argumentation about a topic, which can be very removed from the topic (e.g., mitochondria functioning). There is always the possibility to develop ones own sentiment analyzer, in order to explain it perfectly, but the computational linguists can do a much better job and so I looked to answer the questions with what was available to them. This was essentially the same reason I used an existing API, rather than create a new one. One thing that could be done would be to use a tool like IFEEL, which takes something like 20 of the commonly utilized sentiment analyzers together, allowing many opinions at once.

A related issue to operationalizing the conflict is how to best operationalize the attention or outcome measures. In my studies I examined five or six different outcome measures (Academic, General, and Media attention, number of Tweets on a topic, number of keywords, how often each is utilized), and at least three different types of data (comments on papers, Tweets, and Keywords on papers), but there are literally dozens more options that one could have utilized. Are these the only outcome variables where cognitive conflict demonstrates itself? The suggestion would be no but until one also shows that longer scientific discussions on Facebook, Mendeley, Wikipedia, and Reddit (at least the data sources available from Altmetrics) one will need to be at least a little hestitant to suggest that conflict always leads to positive outcomes for the papers involved.

When focusing on how to improve the way science is done, it is important to focus not only on *how* we answer our questions, but also on asking better questions in the first place.

This dissertation sets a foundation upon which to assert that better understanding cognitive conflict within science can be a way to improve the efficiency of science, both for the individual and for the group at large (Buttliere, 2014).

5.0 Conclusion

Scientists are human, and at least some of the psychological principles which apply to humans also apply to scientists. Here I investigated specifically two ways cognitive conflict demonstrates itself within the scientific enterprise, finding evidence that scientists informally communicate more when they disagree, and that they write more papers about negatively laden topics (e.g., disease, stress) than positively laden topics (e.g., love, encouragement). The implications of these results are substantial. While cognitive conflict is often something that is explicitly avoided by scientists, one might suggest that cognitive conflict is not such a bad thing, even reminding them that many of the greatest thinkers explicitly discuss how important it is to thinking clearly and the scientific process (e.g., Socratic Method, Hegelian Dialectic).

6.0 Statement of work and acknowledgments

This work would not be possible without the input and suggestions of many people. While most of the work was done by myself, especially in conceptualizing, realizing, and writing, many other individuals contributed important pieces of the whole, from providing data, to running analyses and giving suggestions on the structure and form of the writing in the dissertation itself. Peter Holtz ran the LIWC sentiment analysis on the PLoS Comments and the Psych Keywords, as it is a commercial product I do not have access to. Similarly, Rodrigo Costas provided the actual Tweets for the analysis in Study 2. Obviously the microfield structure was provided by Waltman and Eck (2012), as well as the development of the sentiment analysis tools by Hu and Liu (2004), Pennebaker et al., (2015), and Thelwall et al., (2015). But more related, the initial analyses were drafted and run by my favorite research assistant, Kseniia Zviagintseva, utilizing as a template the analyses in the fourth study (sentiment of keywords in psychology), which were developed by myself.

Jürgen Buder and Sonja Utz provided, as the main advisors of the dissertation, feedback on the development and execution of the ideas, also in providing feedback on the structure and form of the content in the thesis. Rather than developing the plan or ideas for me, I believe both advisors would suggest I had plans, and that their contributions lay more in helping to pick the best ones, rather than generate the ideas themselves. Peter Holtz and Rodrigo Costas provided similar feedback on the projects they were a part of, while Seren Yenikent, the entirety of the Knowledge Exchange Lab, the IWM in general, and those individuals I presented to at conferences in general (see the related presentations section) provided general feedback at the indicated presentations. There was also critical proofreading, especially in terms of APA style and references again from Kseniia Zviagintseva and Seren Yenikent, with other general proofing suggestions from e.g., Jürgen Buder and Sonja Utz.

General acknowledgements should be given, especially to Jürgen Buder, for initially hiring me, continuing to pay me while I worked on the project, and being an everyday advisor over the past three years, and Sonja Utz for being willing to participate as the second advisor on my PhD and generally being supportive and giving great feedback in such a timely manner. Thanks are also for Ulrike Cress, Friedrich Hesse, and Rene Ziegler for serving on the dissertation committee and general advice and mentorship.

My friends and Family, especially my Parents, Beth and Tom, my Aunt Gina, My Grandfather, Pops (aka Norbert), All of my family really, Klaus, Simon; Jonas, Larissa, Max, Lukas, Nina, Dr. Koeltzow, Jelte, and many more, for being examples I can follow, and for reminding me that I am also an example for others. Deserved thanks to Seren Yenikent for her support and adventures during this time, and to the entire University and Town of Tübingen for making it such an excellent chapter of my life. To many more adventures and successes!

Table 18 in Study 4 is displayed directly from Ortony and Turner (1990) and utilized as the dataset for the final analyses in Study 4.

Finally, thank You for reading and being here!

The end.

7.0 Works Cited

Adie, E. (2009). Commenting on scientific articles (PLoS edition). B*logs, Nature.* Retrieved from

http://blogs.nature.com/wp/nascent/2009/02/commenting_on_scientific_artic.html.

Altmetrics (2016). The Altmetric top 100: *What Academic Research Caught The Public Imagination in 2015?* Retrieved from https://www.altmetric.com/top100/2015/#

Barber, B. (1961). Resistance by scientists to scientific discovery. *Science, 134*(3479), 596-602.

Baumeister, R. F., Bratslavsky, E., Finkenauer, C., & Vohs, K. D. (2001). Bad is stronger than good. *Review of General Psychology, 5*(4), 323.

Beveridge, W. I. B. (1951). *Art of Scientific Investigation.* Melbourne, Australia, William Heinemann Ltd.

Birukou A., Wakeling J. R., Bartolini C., Casati F., Marchese M., Mirylenka K., et al. (2011). Alternatives to peer review: novel approaches for research evaluation. *Frontiers in Computational Neuroscience 5:*56 10.3389/fncom.2011.00056

Björk B.-C. (2007). A model of scientific communication as a global distributed information system. *Inf. Res. 12:*307 Retrieved from: http://InformationR.net/ir/12-2/paper307.html

Boucher, J., & Osgood, C.E. (1969*).* The pollyanna hypothesis. *Journal of Verbal Learning and Verbal Behavior, 8*(1), 1-8. https://doi.org/10.1016/S0022-5371(69)80002-2

Buttliere, B. (2014). Using science and psychology to improve the dissemination and evaluation of scientific work. *Frontiers in Computational Neuroscience, 8.*

Buttliere, B. & Buder, J. (2015a). Identifying high impact scientific work using natural language processing and psychology. *Quantifying and Analyzing Scholarly Communication on the Web (ASCW'15)*, 1-4.

Buttliere, B., (2015b). We need informative metrics that will help, not hurt, the scientific endeavor – let's work to make metrics better. *London School of Economics Impact of the Social Sciences Blog.* Retrieved from: http://blogs.lse.ac.uk/impactofsocialsciences/2015/10/08/we-need-informative-metrics-how-to-make-metrics-better/

Buttliere, B. (2017). A psychological science: The hidden dependencies of Altmetrics. *Presented at the Workshop on the Dependencies of Altmetrics, at the 4AM conference, Toronto, Canada.*

Buttliere, B. (Submitted A). The role of cognitive conflict in the scientific enterprise. *Social Epistemology,* special issue on the psychology of science.

Buttliere, B., & Buder, J. (2017). Personalizing papers using Altmetrics: comparing paper 'Quality'or 'Impact'to person 'Intelligence'or 'Personality'. *Scientometrics, 111*(1), 219-239.

Buttliere, B., & Buder, J. (2017). Psychologists study more negative topics, more often. *Presented at 10th Conference of theMedia Psychology Division, DGPs, Landau Germany.*

Buttliere, B., Buder, J., & Costas, R., (2017). More discussed scientific topics are more contradicted. *4AM Almetrics Conference*, Toronto, Canada.

Buttliere, B., & Wicherts, J., (2013). What next for scientific communication? A large scale survey of psychologists on problems and potential solutions. Retrieved from https://osf.io/zcv7e/

Byrne, D. E. (1971). *The Attraction Paradigm* (Vol. 11). New York, New York. Academic Press.

Caldin, E. F. (1940). The functions of science. *Nature, 146*, 403-403.

Campanario, J. (2009). Rejecting and resisting Nobel class discoveries: Accounts by Nobel Laureates. *Scientometrics, 81*(2), 549-565.

Camus, A. (1955). *The Myth of Sisyphus, and Other Essays*. New York, New York: Vintage.

Castillo, C.; El-Haddad, M.; Pfeffer, J.; and Stempeck, M. 2014. Characterizing the life cycle of online news stories using social media reactions. In Proceedings of CSCW.

Chen, C., Ibekwe-SanJuan, F., SanJuan, E., & Weaver, C. (2006, October). Visual analysis of conflicting opinions. In *Visual Analytics Science And Technology, 2006 IEEE Symposium On* (pp. 59-66). IEEE.

Chmiel, A., Sobkowicz, P., Sienkiewicz, J., Paltoglou, G., Buckley, K., Thelwall, M., & Hołyst, J. A. (2011). Negative emotions boost user activity at BBC forum. Physica A: Statistical Mechanics and its Applications, 390(16), 2936-2944.

Cosmides, L., & Tooby, J. (2000). Evolutionary psychology and the emotions. *Handbook of Emotions, 2*, 91-115.

Costas, R., Zahedi, Z., & Wouters, P. (2015). Do "altmetrics" correlate with citations? Extensive comparison of altmetric indicators with citations from a multidisciplinary perspective. *Journal of the Association for Information Science and Technology, 66*(10), 2003-2019.

Diamond, E. (1978). Good news, bad news. Cambridge, MA: MIT Press.

Evans, J. S. B., & Stanovich, K. E. (2013). Dual-process theories of higher cognition: Advancing the debate. *Perspectives on psychological science, 8*(3), 223-241.

Feist, G. J., & Gorman, M. E. (1998). The psychology of science: Review and integration of a nascent discipline. *Review of General Psychology, 2*(1), 3.

Feist, G. J., & Gorman, M. E. (Eds.). (2012). *Handbook of the Psychology of Science.* Springer Publishing Company.

Festinger, L. (1950). Informal social communication. *Psychological Review, 57*(5), 271.

Festinger, L. (1954). A theory of social comparison processes. *Human Relations, 7*(2), 117-140.

Festinger, L. (1962). *A Theory of Cognitive Dissonance* (Vol. 2). California, USA. Stanford University Press.

Feyerabend, P. (1970). *Against method: Outline of an Anarchistic Theory of Knowledge.* University of Minnesota Press.

Fiske, S. T. (1980). Attention and weight in person perception: The impact of negative and extreme behavior. *Journal of Personality and Social Psychology, 38*(6), 889.

Giner-Sorolla, R. (2012).Science or Art? How Aesthetic Standards Grease the Way Through the Publication Bottleneck but Undermine Science. *Perspectives on Psychological Science* 7(6), S.562-571. doi: 10.1177/1745691612457576

Gorman, M. E., (1984). A comparison of disconfirmatory, confirmatory and control strategies on Wason's 2–4–6 task. *The Quarterly Journal of Experimental Psychology, 36*(4), 629-648.

Greenwald, A. G., Pratkanis, A. R., Leippe, M. R., & Baumgardner, M. H. (1986). Under what conditions does theory obstruct research progress? *Psychological Review, 93*(2), 216.

Hancock, J.T., Landrigan, C., & Silver, C. (2007). Expressing emotion in text-based communication. *Proceedings of the SIGCHI Conference on Human Factors in Computing Systems*, 929-932. doi>10.1145/1240624.1240764

Hart, W., Albarracín, D., Eagly, A. H., Brechan, I., Lindberg, M. J., & Merrill, L. (2009). Feeling validated versus being correct: a meta-analysis of selective exposure to information. *Psychological Bulletin, 135*(4).

Hegel, G. W. F. (1807). *Phenomenology of Spirit.* Germany. Motilal Banarsidass Publishing.

Heidegger, M., Stambaugh, J., & Schmidt, D. J. (2010). *Being and Time.* New York, New York; SUNY Press.

Heider, F. (2013). *The Psychology of Interpersonal Relations.* Psychology Press.

Heine, S. J., Proulx, T., & Vohs, K. D. (2006). The meaning maintenance model: On the coherence of social motivations. *Personality and Social Psychology Review, 10*(2), 88-110.

Holtz, P., Deutschmann, E., & Dobewall, H. (2017). Cross-Cultural Psychology and the Rise of Academic Capitalism: Linguistic Changes in CCR and JCCP Articles, 1970-2014. *Journal of Cross-Cultural Psychology, 48*(9), 1410-1431.

Hornik, R., Risenhoover, N., & Gunnar, M. (1987). The effects of maternal positive, neutral, and negative affective communications on infant responses to new toys. *Child Development*, 937-944.

Ioannidis, J. P. (2005). Why most published research findings are false. *PLoS Medicine, 18*(4), 40-47.

Kahneman, D. (2011). *Thinking, Fast and Slow*. New York, New York. Macmillan.

Kahneman, D., & Tversky, A. (1979). Prospect theory: An analysis of decision under risk. *Econometrica,* 47(2), 263–292.

Klayman, J., Ha, Y-w. (1989). Hypothesis Testing in Rule Discovery: Strategy, Structure, and Content. *Journal of Experimental Psychology: Learning, Memory, and Cognition*, Vol **15(4), 596**-604.

Koffka, K. (2013). *Principles of Gestalt Psychology* (Vol. 44). Abingdon, United Kingdom: Routledge.

Kraker, P., Lex, E., Gorraiz, J., Gumpenberger, C., & Peters, I. (2015). Research data explored II: The anatomy and reception of figshare. *arXiv preprint arXiv:1503.01298.*

Kramer, A. D., Guillory, J. E., & Hancock, J. T. (2014).Experimental evidence of massive-scale emotional contagion through social networks. *Proceedings of the National Academy of Sciences of the United States of America, 111,* **8788-8790.** 10.1073/pnas.1320040111

Kuhn, T. S. (1962). *The Structure of Scientific Revolutions.* Chicago, IL, USA: University of

    Chicago Press.

LeBel, E. P., Loving, T. J., Campbell, L., (2015). Scrutinizing the Costs versus Benefits of

    Open Science Practices.Retrieved from:

    https://www.researchgate.net/profile/Lorne_Campbell/publication/283018459_LeBel_

    Loving_Campbell_revision/links/5626d08908ae4d9e5c4d47d8.pdf

Lengauer, G., Esser, F., & Berganza, R. (2012). Negativity in political news: A review of

    concepts, operationalizations and key findings. *Journalism, 13*(2), 179-202.

Liu, B., Hu, M., & Cheng, J. (2005, May). Opinion observer: analyzing and comparing

    opinions on the web. *In Proceedings of the 14th international conference on World

    Wide Web (pp. 342-351). ACM.*

Maslow, A. H. (1966). *The Psychology of Science: A Reconnaissance.* Maurice Bassett.

Mahoney, M. J. (1976). *Scientist as Subject: The Psychological Imperative.* Cambridge

    Massachuttes: Ballinger Publishing Company.

Mahoney, M. J. (1977). Publication prejudices: An experimental study of confirmatory bias in

    the peer review system. *Cognitive Therapy and Tesearch,1*(2), 161-175.

Merton, R. K. (1968). The Matthew effect in science. *Science, 159*(3810), 56-63.

Moscovici, S. (2001). *Social Representations: Essays in Social Psychology.* New York, New

    York: NYU Press.

Nesse, R. M. (1990). Evolutionary explanations of emotions. *Human Nature, 1*(3), 261-289.

Nickerson, R. S. (1998). Confirmation bias: A ubiquitous phenomenon in many

guises. *Review of General Psychology, 2*(2), 175-220. http://dx.doi.org/10.1037/1089-

2680.2.2.175

Niven, D. (2001). Bias in the news: Partisanship and negativity in media coverage of

presidents George Bush and Bill Clinton. *Harvard International Journal of

Press/Politics, 6*(3), 31-46.

Open Science Collaboration. (2015). Estimating the reproducibility of psychological

science. *Science, 349*(6251), aac4716.

Osborne, J. (2010). Arguing to learn in science: The role of collaborative, critical discourse.

Science, 328(5977), 463-466.

Öhman, A., Lundqvist, D., & Esteves, F. (2001). The face in the crowd revisited: a threat

advantage with schematic stimuli. *Journal of Personality and Social

Psychology, 80*(3), 381.

Pennebaker, J. W., Francis, M. E., & Booth, R. J. (2001). Linguistic inquiry and word count:

LIWC 2001. *Mahway: Lawrence Erlbaum Associates, 71*(2001), 2001.

Piaget, J. (1955). *The Construction of Reality in the Child* (Vol. 82). Abingdon, United

Kingdom: Routledge.

Platt, J. R. (1964). Strong inference. *Science, 146*(3642), 347-353.

Popper, K. (2005). *The Logic of Scientific Discovery*. Abingdon, United Kingdom: Routledge.

Priem, J., Piwowar, H. A., & Hemminger, B. M. (2012). Altmetrics in the Wild: Using social

media to explore scholarly impact. *arXiv:1203.4745.*

Radicchi, F. (2012). In science "there is no bad publicity": Papers criticized in comments have

    high scientific impact. *Scientific Reports, 2*.

Sartre, J.P. (1943). *Being and Nothingness*. Open Road Media, 2012.

Schwarz, N. (1990). *Feelings as Information: Informational and Motivational Functions of*

    Affective States. New York, New York: Guilford Press.

Seligman, M. E., & Csikszentmihalyi, M. (2014). Positive psychology: An introduction.

    In *Flow and the Foundations of Positive Psychology* (pp. 279-298). New York, New

    York: Springer

Sen, S., & Lerman, D. (2007). Why are you telling me this? An examination into negative

    consumer reviews on the web. *Journal of Interactive Marketing, 21*(4), 76-94.

Sendhilkumar, S., Elakkiya, E., & Mahalakshmi, G. S. (2013). Citation semantic based

    approaches to identify article quality. In *Proceedings of International Conference*

    ICCSEA, 411-420.

Simmons, J. P., Nelson, L. D., & Simonsohn, U. (2011). False-positive psychology:

    Undisclosed flexibility in data collection and analysis allows presenting anything as

    significant. *Psychological Science, 22*(11), 1359-1366.

Sobkowicz, P., & Sobkowicz, A. (2012). Two-year study of emotion and communication

    patterns in a highly polarized political discussion forum. *Social Science Computer*

    Review, 30(4), 448-469.

Soroka, S., & McAdams, S. (2015). News, politics, and negativity. *Political*

    Communication, 32(1), 1-22.

Stent, G. S. (1972). Prematurity and uniqueness in scientific discovery.*Scientific American, 227*, 84-93.

Sterne, J. A., Egger, M., & Moher, D. (2008). Addressing reporting biases.*Cochrane Handbook for Systematic Reviews of Interventions: Cochrane Book Series*, 297-333.

Thelwall, M., Buckley, K., & Paltoglou, G. (2012). Sentiment strength detection for the social web. Journal of the Association for Information Science and Technology, 63(1), 163-173.

Tversky, A., & Kahneman, D. (1971). Belief in the law of small numbers. *Psychological Bulletin, 76*(2), 105.

Tversky, A., & Kahneman, D. (1985). The framing of decisions and the psychology of choice. In *Environmental Impact Assessment, Technology Assessment, and Risk Analysis* (pp. 107-129). Berlin, Germany: Springer.

Tversky, A., & Kahneman, D. (1991). Loss aversion in riskless choice: A reference dependent model. *Quarterly Journal of Economics, 41*, 1039–1061.

van Schijndel, T. J., Visser, I., van Bers, B. M., & Raijmakers, M. E. (2015). Preschoolers perform more informative experiments after observing theory-violating evidence. *Journal of Experimental Child Psychology*, 131, 104-119.

Wason, P. C. (1960). On the failure to eliminate hypotheses in a conceptual task. *Quarterly Journal of Experimental Psychology, 12*(3), 129-140.

Web of Knowledge (2017). Web of Science Quick Reference Guide. Accessed, October 16, 2017. Retrieved from: http://wokinfo.com/media/pdf/qrc/webofscience_qrc_en.pdf

Wikipedia (2017). List of countries by research and development spending. Retrieved from:

    https://en.wikipedia.org/wiki/List_of_countries_by_research_and_development_spend

    ing